Mrs.
L B J

RUTH MONTGOMERY

Mrs.

LBJ

HOLT, RINEHART AND WINSTON

NEW YORK · CHICAGO · SAN FRANCISCO

Published simultaneously in Canada by Holt,
Rinehart and Winston of Canada, Limited.

Library of Congress Catalog Card Number:
64-15307

Published, March, 1964
Second Printing, April, 1964
Third Printing, April, 1964

Designer: Ernst Reichl
85789-0114
Printed in the United States of America

To my mother,
Bertha Judy Shick,
whose encouragement and love have been
as unceasing as
Lady Bird Johnson's unflagging devotion
to her husband, the President.

Foreword

MY ADMIRATION for the reporter who goes her daily rounds to cover the news is excelled only by my esteem for one who also has the discipline, energy, and talent to write a book.

Such is the gift of Ruth Montgomery whose by-line I have long admired and whose friendship I have long appreciated.

It is a new experience to be the subject of a book. The opportunity to write an introduction to one's own biography is an even more novel courtesy. I confess, however, that the experiment has been painless and that these pages have jogged recollections both poignant and pleasant.

I hope those who read it will enjoy reading it as much as I enjoyed living it.

Lady Bird Johnson

Mrs.
L B J

Chapter

1

THOMAS JEFFERSON TAYLOR hunched his broad shoulders and gazed fondly down from his towering six-feet-two at the petite brunette daughter by his side. The time was November 16, 1934. The place was the front parlor of historic "Brick House," an ante-bellum manor house on an East Texas cotton plantation, whose bricks had been hand-baked by slaves on the site.

The young Southern belle returned his look in hushed expectancy. Love for her only living parent so obviously glowed in the deep wells of her dark brown eyes that, after a brief pause which seemed an eternity, the big man drawled, "If you wait 'til your Aunt Effie's really ready, you'll never marry anybody."

With those judicious words, Thomas Jefferson Taylor, "Dealer in Everything," not only gave his blessing to the marriage of twenty-one-year-old Lady Bird but may also have changed the course of history.

Who, on that crisp November day, could have foreseen that with a ten-thousand-dollar loan against her inheritance, the open-hearted young woman would one day finance her husband's first campaign for Congress, a campaign which would eventually lead him to the presidency?

Aunt Effie Pattillo lay ailing in an Alabama hospital. Although the lanky, wavy-haired Congressional secretary was ardently pressing Lady Bird Taylor to give him an answer to his proposal of marriage, she felt a deep obligation to the spinster aunt who had reared her from the age of six.

"I simply have to go see Aunt Effie first," she had told her eager suitor with quiet finality. "With no husband or children of her own, she has concentrated all her life and love on me—more, probably, than was good for either of us."

The lonely journey to Alabama tore at her heart. Aunt Effie was as fragile as a Dresden doll, and equally as unworldly. "Oh, it was a fearsome thing I had to do," the First Lady now sighs. "It was just as though I had stepped on a Cape Jasmine, because I knew that it would hurt her. Not only would I be leaving her, but I would be taking the very hazardous step of marrying a strange male whom I had known less than two months."

Aunt Effie predictably tried to discourage her beloved Lady Bird. Over and again she kept repeating the old adage: "If he loves you as much as he says he does, he'll wait for you."

Now the grievously torn young woman was back at the "Brick House," where Lyndon Baines Johnson impatiently waited, unwilling to accept anything except an immediate *yes* for an answer. He and Mr. Taylor had had a man-to-man talk during Lady Bird's absence, and it was apparent that the older man considered him a highly acceptable son-in-law.

"Some of the best deals are made in a hurry," her father said laconically, but she was not quite sure. In an agony of indecision the gently reared young woman at last agreed to let Lyndon drive her to the home of her closest friend in Austin. The next morning she tremulously packed a suitcase, and as the automobile sped along through the flat Texas prairie, the young-man-in-a-hurry persisted: "We either do it now or we never will. If you say good-bye to me, it just proves that you don't love me enough to dare. I simply can't bear to go back to Washington and keep on wondering if it will ever happen."

Lady Bird realized the hazards of a hasty marriage perhaps more than did her impetuous suitor. She had re-read the Episcopal marriage ceremony only the day before, and as gently as possible she asked if he understood what all of those promises entailed. Lyndon admitted that he had never read the service, but he was willing to promise anything to have Lady Bird forever at his side.

Musing thoughtfully, the First Lady now says: "Simply because I didn't want to let him go either, we were married at seven o'clock that evening of November 17th at St. Mark's Episcopal Church in San Antonio. Austin held too many school-day memories. I didn't want to be married there."

Lyndon Baines Johnson has always known how to get things done. While his bride-to-be telephoned a college roommate, Cecile Harrison, to come and stand up with her,

Lyndon asked his friend, Postmaster Dan Quill, to arrange for the church and the preacher. Although Lyndon belonged to the Christian Church, Bird was an Episcopalian, and they settled on historic St. Mark's.

As the simple ceremony was about to begin, the "can-do" bridegroom suddenly realized that he had forgotten the ring. Bird was already wearing the engagement ring he had purchased in Austin, but there was no time now to secure a matching band. The obliging postmaster sprinted across the street to Sears, Roebuck and scooped up a dozen rings for size.

The one that fit cost $2.98, and Lyndon proudly slipped it on Lady Bird's finger as the Rt. Reverend Arthur McKinstry solemnly intoned: "With this ring I thee wed."

Reverend McKinstry, later to become Bishop of Delaware, confesses that he had been reluctant to perform the ceremony, because the young couple seemed in such a hurry. Even then, however, it was difficult to refuse Lyndon anything, and romance won over pastoral reservations.

Reverend McKinstry pronounced the young couple man and wife, and after Lyndon had swept his bride into his arms, they set off in the car that he was buying on the installment plan for a honeymoon in Mexico.

The inseparable team of Lady Bird and Lyndon Baines Johnson had now been joined. Neither could have believed that the White House lay ahead.

Chapter

2

LADY BIRD is not, of course, her real name. Christened Claudia Alta Taylor, she was delivered by country doctor Benjamin Baldwin early on a chill December morning in 1912, while every fireplace in the big old mansion crackled cheerfully through the night.

The nearest town was Karnack, which had been named by some culturally-minded pioneer for the Karnak ruins of ancient Thebes in upper Egypt, but haplessly misspelled.

Claudia was such a dainty little thing that her Negro nursemaid said she was "as purty as a Lady Bird." Big, bluff Thomas Jefferson Taylor thought so too, and from then on everyone called her that, until friends eventually shortened it to "Bird."

The First Lady vaguely remembers her mother as a "tall, graceful woman who wore white quite a lot, and went around the house in a great rush." The former Minnie Pattillo, daughter of an aristocratic Alabama family, loved to read, and despite her raw frontier surroundings in East Texas, she had amassed an impressive collection of books.

The shelves of the paneled library groaned with tomes: histories, biographies, twenty volumes of the world's greatest classics, a set of the *Book of Knowledge*, the H. Rider Haggard series on the occult, all of Voltaire's works, and such familiar children's stories as *Tom Sawyer, Huckleberry Finn*, and the Zane Grey adventure series. These were to provide the foundation for Lady Bird's education; they also help to explain her quaint turn of phrase today.

Intellectual, wealthy Minnie Pattillo had married Tom Taylor against the wishes of her father. Luke Pattillo was a patrician man of Spanish and Scottish descent, and was a worthy representative of Alabama's "first family." The Taylors were of English extraction, but although they were landowners, they had failed to impress the neighbors with their farming ability.

In defiance of her father, Minnie sometimes rode her blooded saddle horse to the Taylor farm, and eventually she married Tom. Like many another young bridegroom at the turn of the century, he then set out for Texas to seek their fortune, and later brought his bride to the frontier country near Karnack.

Two sons—Tom, Junior, and Antonio—were born there, and after another eight years, a baby girl named Claudia. Perhaps the cultural isolation was a contributing factor, but while the future First Lady was still a toddler, her mother suffered a nervous breakdown. "Miss Minnie," as the adoring servants called her, went for a time to a hospital in Battle Creek, Michigan, but soon recovered and returned to the "Brick House."

"I remember Mother only vaguely," the First Lady says. "She used to read me Greek, Roman and Teutonic myths. Siegfried was the first romantic hero I ever loved."

Lady Bird's mother became pregnant again. One afternoon, as she was ascending the circular staircase, the family collie bounded between her feet, and Mrs. Taylor plunged the full length of the stairs. She was rushed to the county hospital because of a miscarriage, and a few days later Lady Bird was taken there to see her. It was the last time. Blood poisoning had set in, and on September 14, 1918, her forty-four-year-old mother died.

Reflecting on that long-ago tragedy, the First Lady says: "As I look back on Mother's death I am terrifically sorry for Daddy, and quite sorry for my two brothers. They were thirteen and sixteen at the time, and their lives were adversely affected by the sudden pulling away of a woman who would have seen that they received good educations.

"But I don't feel in the least sorry for myself. At five, one is pretty much insulated from pain. Besides, I was quite sure that she was going to come back. I could hear people saying that Mother was gone. I could tell that they were feeling sorry for me, but I thought to myself, 'Well, I know more about that than they do. She'll be back.' But as time went on, I quit even thinking about it. It may have been some sort of protective cloak that nature puts around young folks, but I never thought of myself as having a lonely childhood."

Lady Bird's closest companions in her pre-school years were the Negro children of the washerwoman and the sharecroppers. It was a semifeudal way of life in those prewar days of the Old South, and Cotton was King. Tom Taylor had two cotton gins and a general store in the nearby village of Karnack. A sign above the door read: "T. J. Taylor, Dealer in Everything." Tenant farmers sharecropped his land, raising corn, hogs, and vegetables for the table, but pouring most of their sweat and toil into the money crop: cotton.

From September until Christmas after her mother's death, Lady Bird's father needed to be close to his business. This was his busiest season, when cotton had to be ginned and Negroes flocked to the store to pay up their accounts and spend their yearly profits.

"Fall was the financial high point of our year," Lady Bird explains. "This was the time when we would go to the bank to pay off our loans, and use the rest of the money to buy adjoining land—always the land next to us—from the neighbor who wanted to give up farming and move to town." As the years passed, Tom Taylor gradually came to own the entire north end of the county, encompassing several thousand acres.

Lady Bird remembers her father as a tall, handsome man who was "a very strong character, to put it mildly." He lived by his own rules, and that fall, after her mother's death, he took a practical step that somewhat shocked the kinfolks. Since he had to stay at the store long past midnight, and his little daughter was too young to be left at the plantation without parental supervision, he put up a bed for her in the warehouse over the store.

Smiling reminiscently, she says: "The first night I saw a row of peculiar long boxes near my bed and asked Daddy what they were. I noticed that he hesitated a moment before replying, 'Dry goods, honey.' " The countryside abounded with ghost stories, and the little girl had been generously exposed to them by the cook and washer-woman. Her father sensibly chose to tell her a fib, because the long boxes were empty coffins.

At Christmastime that year, the adult kinfolks "put their heads together" and decided that the big old manor house was no place for a little girl to be alone, since her father had to be gone so much of the time and her older brothers were away at prep schools. They consequently settled on Aunt Effie Pattillo, an unmarried younger sister of Lady Bird's mother, as the most available chaperon.

Lady Bird adored the blonde, blue-eyed, ethereal woman who came from Alabama to preside over her formative years. Aunt Effie doted on taking long walks in the woods, watching the vivid Texas sunrises over the misty cotton fields, and encouraging the imaginative little girl to create make-believe friends.

"She was undoubtedly the most other-worldly human in the world," the First Lady says fondly. "She was delicate and airy and very gentle, and she gave me many fine values which I wouldn't trade for the world. She had the polite musical education considered proper for a young lady of her day, and she played the piano quite well. She was, how-ever, always thinking of others, and was a great hand to look after all the needy members of the family and the community."

One thing that would never have occurred to the un-sophisticated little spinster was "trying to choose a young-ster's friends, seeing that a little girl went to the proper dancing school, or that she had a dress a little nicer than Mary Jones'." As a result, Lady Bird feels that she herself looks at material values "through a double set of eyeglasses."

Lady Bird often accompanied her nurse and playmates to their Negro church, and considered it exciting, although she regularly attended the Methodist one where her own family gathered to worship. Educational facilities were segregated by long-established Southern custom, however, and she attended a one-room country school on a red clay hill near the plantation. The number of pupils varied considerably, depending on how many tenant farmers were currently working the fields. Three months before school recessed one spring, a sharecropper with a good many children moved away, and the enrollment dropped to one —Lady Bird Taylor.

"Oh, how I loved that one-room schoolhouse," the First Lady rhapsodizes. "It's a vanished American institution now, but I like to tell my children tales about it. There was a plump stove in the middle of the room, and the big boys always brought in the wood, and started the fire going on cool mornings. Every Friday afternoon we had what the teacher called 'exercises.' We sang patriotic songs which we had learned verse by verse. I went there from the first grade through the seventh."

During the summers Lady Bird and Aunt Effie traveled to Colorado and Michigan, but always went back to Alabama for carefree vacations with their kinfolks. Uncle Claude Pattillo, her mother's bachelor brother for whom she was named, was a food faddist who sternly watched her diet. He also encouraged her to read thick books on finance, and taught her to study stock-market quotations before she was twelve.

Uncle Claude dreamed of his bright young niece going

to the Harvard School of Business, and although she never did, the interest he awakened at this time was later to prove of inestimable value when she inherited vast tracts of Alabama farmland from him, Aunt Effie, and her mother.

Lady Bird was an apt pupil, and after completing elementary school, she transferred to Jefferson for two years, and then eighteen miles down the dirt road to the high school at Marshall, the county seat. She was only thirteen, but she drove her own car to school and back, and even to Alabama during vacations. Learning was easy for her. She was a straight A student, and as high-school graduation neared, it became apparent that she was "perilously" close to having the best grades in her class. The very thought of delivering the valedictorian or salutatorian address appalled her. Desperately shy, she decided that she would "just as soon have the smallpox as open my mouth" before the doting parental audience.

She therefore began to pray that Emma Boehringer, one of her closest friends, would be named valedictorian, and Maurine Kranson salutatorian. She desperately wanted to come in third, however, because she had enough pride to value achievement, although not enough courage to speak.

The year ended in a near photo finish. Emma had a 95 average, Maurine a 94.5, and Lady Bird 94. Paradoxically, the young girl who could not bear to make a speech in high-school has since become the best feminine campaigner in the Democratic stable.

Lady Bird, like her future husband, graduated from high school at the age of fifteen. Lyndon had not wanted to continue his studies and had set off with some neighboring lads on a hitchhiking trip to California after graduation, but Lady Bird could scarcely wait to enroll at St. Mary's School for Girls, an Episcopal junior college in Dallas. It was due to that influence that she later changed her church affiliation from Methodist to Episcopalian, and after graduation she went to Austin to visit Gene Boehringer, a sister of Emma's.

"I fell in love with Austin the first moment that I laid eyes on it," Lady Bird recalls, "and that love has never slackened. It's a wonderful town, and Gene was one of those tremendously out-going people who made everyone around her feel a little more alive. You kind of waited for her to come in the room. She always thought of interesting things to do, and I am a friendlier and more confident person today because of my friendship with Gene."

It was mainly because of Gene that Lady Bird decided to continue her college education at the University of Texas in Austin. Pretty Miss Taylor had no more scholastic difficulty in the big State University than she had had at Marshall High. She earned a bachelor of arts degree in 1933 and then, because there was no hurry for the young heiress to find a job, she stayed another year to acquire a bachelor's degree in journalism.

Bird Taylor graduated in the top ten per cent of her class, but she was never considered a bookworm. She had her own Buick at school, in the depression days when few campus students were so privileged, and unlimited use of her father's checkbook. She joined several campus societies —although not a social sorority because Tom Taylor disapproved of them—and she served as secretary of Theta Sigma Phi, the women's honorary journalism fraternity.

For a graduation present her proud father gave her a trip to Washington, D.C. Her destiny was almost at hand.

Chapter

3

GENE BOEHRINGER was a born matchmaker. As soon as she learned that Lady Bird and her roommate, Cecile Harrison, were planning a trip to Washington that fateful summer of 1934, she exclaimed: "Wonderful! I know just the man for you to meet. He's a good friend of mine, and I'll write him that you're coming. I'll jot down his name and phone number for you and tell him to expect you. Be sure to call him as soon as you get there, and he'll be delighted to show you the sights of the capital."

The shy Southern girl tucked the slip of paper in her purse, but thought no more about it. She and her friend knew several former Texans who lived in Washington, and she had no intention of telephoning a strange young man.

Several weeks later, after returning to Austin, she and

Dorothy Muckleroy were chatting in Gene's office at the state capital when a stranger from Washington strolled in. Fate had taken matters into its own hands. Lady Bird and Lyndon Johnson were at last to meet. While Gene performed the introductions, Bird discreetly looked him over.

"He was excessively thin," she recalls, "but very, very good-looking, with lots of black wavy hair, and the most outspoken, straightforward, determined manner I had ever encountered. I knew I had met something remarkable, but I didn't know quite what."

Lyndon invited the three girls to have a drink with him, and since it was office closing time, they accompanied him to a nearby coffee shop. It soon became apparent that the young man was no time waster. He already had a date with Dorothy for that evening, but he asked Bird to have breakfast with him the following morning in the dining room of the Driskill Hotel.

Dropping her eyes, Bird gave him a noncommittal reply. Unaccustomed to such a bold approach from a stranger, she was nonetheless drawn to him. As she frankly admits: "I was uncertain whether I wanted to have breakfast with him, because I had a queer sort of moth-and-the-flame feeling about what a remarkable man he was."

The twenty-six-year-old Lyndon seemed very much a man of the world to gently-nurtured Lady Bird. He had obviously been around. He knew a lot of important people, and he was the Congressional secretary to Representative Richard Kleberg, a part owner of the almost legendary King Ranch. Even more importantly, Gene liked him, but what should Bird do?

She already had an engagement with architect Hugo Kuehne the next morning. Now that her college days were behind her, Tom Taylor had asked his only daughter to superintend the restoration of their lovely old "Brick House." She had to concede that Mr. Kuehne's office was convenient to the meeting place that Lyndon had suggested. It was next door to the hotel. The following morning, as she arrived for her appointment with the architect, she shyly refrained from glancing into the hotel dining room which opened off the street. The temptation was there, however, and on leaving Mr. Kuehne she saw Lyndon through the window.

Says the President: "I was sitting at the front table watching for her, when I saw her come out of the office. I've always doubted whether she would ever have found the courage to walk in there otherwise."

Lyndon had been waiting for some time. They had breakfast together, and then he drove her out into the country in his car. The First Lady vividly recalls his conversation this way: "He told me all sorts of things that I thought were extraordinarily direct for a first date—about how many years he had been teaching, about how much he liked his job as secretary to a Texas Congressman, about all the members of his family, and even how much insurance he carried. It was as if he wanted to give me a complete picture of his life and of his capabilities."

Gradually he drew from his reticent companion a clearer picture of the woman within. In college she had wanted to acquire some tools for making a living, because she knew that restoring the old homestead would not keep her occupied for long. She had seen enough of the world to realize that Karnack held few opportunities for an educated young woman.

She had earned a second-grade teaching certificate, hoping that it would carry her to some "far-off romantic place like Hawaii or Alaska," but she had no real desire to teach. Next, she had taken a typing and shorthand course, because Jean had made her aware that with brains and personality a good secretary could carve out a satisfying career in the business world. It was not until after graduation that she decided journalism was the field for her.

"I thought that newspaper people went more places, and met more interesting people than anyone else," she laughs ruefully now. "Such exciting things seemed always to be happening to them."

The young man was charmed by the soft-spoken but sturdily self-reliant young woman from East Texas. Years later he was to say of her: "She is still the most enjoyable woman I've ever met. As a sweetheart, a swimmer, a rider, and a conversationalist, she is the most interesting woman I know."

The day following their breakfast date Lyndon drove Lady Bird to San Marcos to meet his parents. As this confident eldest son presented her to his mother, Bird could "almost see the uncertainty" in the older woman's face.

"She idolized Lyndon," the First Lady explains, "and I could readily understand the questions flashing through her mind: Was her son seriously interested in this young woman? Is she the right one for him? She was a very great and very devoted mother, but I think maybe Lyndon meant more to her than the other four children, although she would never admit it. I felt so sympathetic toward her that I kept wanting to tell her, 'Don't worry, I'm not trying to run off with this young man.' I knew she was worried about me. What sensible woman wouldn't have been?"

A few days later Lyndon drove Lady Bird to meet his boss, who maintained a home office at the fabulous King ranch which his family owned. Representative Kleberg's mother took an immediate liking to the well-bred young woman, and before the visit ended she was privately advising her to marry Lyndon.

Bird could not help but be impressed, as thousands of other Americans and distinguished foreigners have been, by a visit to this world-famous ranch. It was not only the largest privately held tract of land in the nation, far larger than some states, but it was a feudal domain presided over by an extraordinary family. To Miss Taylor, the mother of the clan seemed "very much the duchess, very much the great lady," and as Bird met each of her sons, she noticed that Lyndon Baines Johnson was highly regarded by them all.

The time had now come for Lyndon to return to his job in Washington, but he could still not bear to let Bird out of his sight. He wanted to meet her father, and since Karnack is on the way from Austin to Washington, he persuaded a friend to bring his car that far so that he could drive Bird in her's.

The miles flew by in a happy confusion of conversation. At last, her Buick turned into the lane leading to the plantation, and Tom Taylor was waiting to greet them. As she introduced the two towering Texans to each other, she could "see that Daddy was impressed right away."

The talk at dinner was general, but in a quiet moment afterward she asked her father what he thought of her ardent young suitor. "Mr. Boss," as the villagers called Tom Taylor, cleared his throat and hmmmmmed: "You've been bringing home a lot of boys. This time you've brought a man."

Lyndon stayed all night. The water pump was not working, and a houseboy went to fetch his bath water from the reservoir. Lyndon could not have been less interested in what went on around him. He had only one thing on his mind—to marry the girl that he loved. He proposed that night, but she needed more time to think it over. Scarcely a week had elapsed since they had met, but as he left for Washington the next morning, she walked with him to the crossroads and let him kiss her good-bye. As soon as he reached the capital he began telephoning her every day.

Smiling nostalgically, Lady Bird muses: "To carry on a courtship over a country telephone is quite a feat. You hear about every third word, and so do the eavesdropping neighbors. We seemed always to be screaming at each other to talk a little louder, and sometimes I would drive into Marshall to take his long-distance call at the home of my friend, Laura Sacral."

Lyndon sent her his photograph, on which he wrote: "For Bird, a girl of principles, ideals and refinement, from her admirer, Lyndon." The letters flew back and forth between them, and in late October he arrived again at the "Brick House."

The seven-weeks separation had heightened his native impatience, and as he held her hand he pleaded: "Let's get married! Not next year, after you've stayed home a year and done over the house, but about two weeks from now— or a month from now—or right away."

His relentless pressure was wearing her down, just as he had hoped that it would. But he had not bargained on Aunt Effie. The elderly spinster was now hospitalized, and the gentle, thoughtful Bird could not bear to make the most important decision of her life without first consulting the unworldly soul who had reared her.

"I simply have to go to Alabama first and ask her opinion," she said with unusual firmness. And she went.

As the President tells the story: "Bird went to see her Aunt Effie who had raised her, and asked her whether she should marry me. Aunt Effie told her not to, and Bird went back to Texas and told her father and me. Her father said the aunt never would agree, and for her to go ahead. We drove to San Antonio, and she still hadn't said yes until we got there. I sent a friend over to buy a ring, and we were married at the Episcopal church on the square."

Now they had the same initials—LBJ—and her real name had been so nearly forgotten that the engraved wedding announcements read: Claudia Alta (Lady Bird) Taylor . . .

Chapter

4

LIFE FOR Mrs. Lyndon Baines Johnson was a decided contrast to life for Claudia Alta Taylor. Instead of presiding over a graceful Southern mansion, she came as a Washington bride to a modest one-bedroom apartment with a roll-away bed in the living room. Instead of an unlimited checking account from an indulgent father, she now had to make ends meet on a Congressional secretary's salary of $267 a month.

Lyndon kept a hundred dollars to cover his lunches; his law-school tuition at George Washington University, which he attended evenings; installment payments on his car, and its upkeep. With the remainder, his wife managed so capably that they bought an $18.75 government bond each payday.

Washington has always been a mecca for tourists, and

so many relatives and friends descended on the struggling young couple that once, for several weeks in a row, Aunt Effie, Lyndon's Uncle George Johnson, and a secretary were sleeping there at the same time. It was to prove good training for the hospitable Johnsons, who in more recent years have entertained twenty or thirty house guests at a time at the LBJ ranch.

As a bride, Lady Bird Johnson had almost everything to learn about housekeeping. Before her marriage she had never swept a floor or cooked a meal. Undismayed, she bought a cookbook and decided that the only trick was learning to have everything ready at once.

Her first dinner guests were Congressman and Mrs. Maury Maverick, old Texas friends of Lyndon's, and she can still remember her menu that evening. It featured baked ham and lemon pie. She had deliberately chosen foods that she could prepare in advance, to avoid missing the "good talk" in the crowded living room.

A cleaning woman came once a week to scrub the floors, but the frugal bride did all the rest of her housework. Deciding that Lyndon did not read enough books and magazines, despite the fact that he had eventually graduated from Southwest State Teachers College in San Marcos, Texas, she began marking important passages in publications of all sorts to call to his attention.

Lyndon was an activist, and his young wife soon understood him well enough to know that he absorbed learning through osmosis rather than study. He was impatient to get ahead in the world. His heart and soul were in the New Deal experiments, and nine months after their marriage he resigned his Capital Hill job to accept an appointment as the Texas State Administrator of the National Youth Administration.

"We moved to Austin, and our house became a beehive of activity," the First Lady recalls. "It was constantly filled with folks who worked for the NYA, or folks who needed jobs, or folks who were just dropping in to give advice. It was a real initiation into what the whole rest of my life was to be."

Thinking back over those hectic eighteen months in Austin, Bird reflects: "I don't know of a comparable time when Lyndon put so much love and so much drive into anything. Man had found job! This was work cut to his cloth—trying to put young people back into schools if they could get part-time work, or teaching them skills and getting them jobs. He has probably never known greater satisfaction than in taking those young hitchhikers off of the boxcars and highways and putting them to use at something productive."

Mary Rather, later to become Lyndon's secretary and the family's confidante, recalls the first time that she met Lady Bird. She and a friend were talking to the NYA Administrator when suddenly he said: "Come on home to dinner with me and meet Bird." The two women were embarrassed at the thought of upsetting his wife, but Lyndon would not take no for an answer. Telephoning Bird to expect two extra guests for dinner, he firmly guided them to his car.

"We had no time to change clothes," Mary recalls, "and we were uneasy about the kind of reception to expect, but that's because we didn't know Lady Bird. She was utterly unperturbed. She was doing all of her own work, but in a little while she had a beautiful steak dinner on the table."

About this time an event occurred that was to change the course of their lives. James Buchanan, the elderly Congressman from that Texas district, died. A special election was scheduled to fill his House seat—and there Lyndon was on the home ground.

Bird thinks that "the seed of running for elective office" had perhaps lain dormant in his mind since boyhood. He had often heard from his parents that on the day of his birth, August 27, 1908, his grandfather boasted to the neighbors: "A United States Senator has been born today."

The young wife was as proud as was Lyndon of his rich political heritage. His father had served six terms in the Texas House of Representatives, part of the time with his good friend, Sam Rayburn, who was later to become Lyndon's political mentor. His paternal grandfather, a Confederate veteran, had also served in the Texas legislature. One of his ancestors signed the Texas Declaration of Independence, and had fought with a squirrel rifle against the Mexicans in 1836.

Now Lyndon's own great opportunity seemed at hand, but his chances were something less than impressive. True, he had made many loyal friends in Austin as the nation's youngest NYA Administrator, but his home county of Blanco was the smallest of the ten in the district. Lyndon gamely faced the facts. He was virtually a stranger in the other counties, the least well known of the ten rivals for the vacant seat, and he had no money for an extensive campaign.

But for Lady Bird, he could not possibly have run. Before the decision had to be made, she went for a walk one Sunday with State Senator Alvin Wirtz, a family friend whose opinion she valued highly. He frankly cautioned her that the campaign would cost ten thousand dollars, and that four or five of the other contestants would have a better chance than Lyndon.

That was good enough for Bird. If Lyndon looked better than the other half of the field, she was willing to gamble her inheritance. Returning from the walk, she placed a long-distance call to the "Brick House" and asked: "Daddy, do you suppose you could put ten thousand dollars in the bank for me? Lyndon wants to run for Congress."

Without a moment's hesitation the doting "Mr. Boss" replied: "Well, today's Sunday. I don't think I could do it before tomorrow morning about nine o'clock."

The money, she knew, would eventually come from her share of her mother's estate, which Tom Taylor had profitably reinvested for her.

"It was a tremendous campaign, and Lyndon was never so young, never so vigorous, and never so wonderful," his wife lovingly recalls. "My only regret is that I didn't have the gumption to share in it, although I suppose it would have looked odd in those days for me to go around campaigning for him. In 1937, it simply wasn't done in Texas."

Vigorous, peripatetic Lyndon ranged up and down the district, campaigning on an all-out Roosevelt New Deal program. The fact that he gave wholehearted support to FDR's controversial court-packing plan quickly paid off. President Roosevelt was then fishing in the Gulf of Mexico off Texas, and when Lyndon won the election, FDR invited him to join him on the presidential train at Galveston.

The intimate, man-to-man talks aboard the slow train were not wasted. After a word from FDR, the freshman legislator won appointment to the House Naval Affairs

Committee. The Navy was President Roosevelt's pet service, and he soon began inviting the neophyte Congressman to breakfast at the White House so that they could talk about it.

With such all-out blessing from the White House, LBJ lacked even an opponent in his re-election campaigns of 1938 and 1940. Everything went smoothly, in fact, until FDR persuaded him to run for the vacant Senate seat of Morris Sheppard, who had died in office in 1941.

A dozen other candidates declared, too, but the race soon narrowed into a hard-fought contest between youthful Representative Johnson and the colorful governor, W. Lee O'Daniel. The latter campaigned with a hillbilly band, and not to be outdone, Lyndon traveled through the Lone Star State with a portly singer called the "Kate Smith of the South."

Johnson was announced the winner, and three thousand congratulatory telegrams poured into his Austin headquarters. Then the majority began dwindling away; and five days later O'Daniel emerged the victor, with a slim margin of 1,311 votes out of a million cast.

Recalling their disappointment, the First Lady says: "A memory of Lyndon that I will always cherish was the way he looked, walking away to catch the plane back to Washington after his defeat had been announced. I still see him striding off, looking very jaunty, and putting extra verve into his step. His head was high, and he was stepping along real spryly. He had thought that he had won, and had practically hired a staff. I knew how much nerve and effort were now required for him to keep up that courageous appearance. But I think the experience was good for him. I can't say that a solid diet of success is good for anybody."

The Nazis were overrunning Europe, and threatening to engulf the entire world in their blood bath. Defeated for the Senate in that special election of June, 1941, the young Congressman returned to his seat in the House and announced that if he had to vote for our entry into war, he would go himself. Less than six months later the vote came. The day following the Japanese attack on Pearl Harbor, Lyndon Johnson was the first member of the House to go on active duty. A member of the Naval Reserve for several years, he was commissioned a lieutenant commander.

During the next seven months, before President Roosevelt issued a directive barring national legislators from serving in the armed forces, Lyndon won the Silver Star on bombing missions in the South Pacific.

No one would have blamed Bird if, during that worrisome period while Lyndon was away at war, she had returned home to live with her father or Aunt Effie. After seven years she was still childless, and she could have written to her husband as easily from East Texas as Washington.

It was then, however, that her unsuspected political know-how began to assert itself. The day after Lyndon departed from Washington in uniform, his wife took over the management of his busy legislative office—without pay. She had never worked there before, as some Congressional wives had, and she was totally without experience in the workaday world, but Bird felt that she, as well as Lyndon, had a mission to perform.

Explaining why she decided to take this unprecedented step, she observes astutely: "Lyndon has always had a marvelous staff, close knit and able, but there's nobody who cares quite as much about your business as yourself, and next to yourself, your wife. I decided to serve because I cared that extra little bit. To put it bluntly, I also realized that I could probably get into a few offices and see a few people that the staff members couldn't, and this was important to Lyndon's constituents."

Bird was justly proud of her husband's political record, and she believed that the people of his district would feel a closer bond to their absent Congressman if his wife served as "a kind of liaison" between them.

The First Lady is convinced that this experience was one of the best things that could have happened to her, because: "After a few months, I really felt that if it was ever necessary, I could make my own living. That's a good feeling to have. You begin to unravel some mysteries and to find out how to do a lot of things. You achieve a little sense of mastery and understanding, which broadens you and makes you a better person."

Continuing with her soul-searching, she says thoughtfully: "The very best part of it was that it gave me a lot more understanding of Lyndon. By the time the end of the day came, when I had shifted the gears in my mind innumerable times, I could know what Lyndon had been through. One moment I would be talking to the Mayor of Austin about the new abattoir the city was trying to build when materials were scarce, and the next I would be taking a phone call from some constitutent whose son was absent or missing in action and his mother was dying."

The constant shifting of thought, and the perpetual concentration proved so tiring that by the end of the day, when she met friends for relaxation, she would "get almost mad at them" if they asked her to decide where they would dine.

It is no secret that Lyndon Baines Johnson is a man of many moods. He is either up in the clouds or down in the dumps, and Bird has had to adjust to his occasional black moods. Of her experience in running his office, she admits: "I was more prepared after that to understand what sometimes had seemed to be Lyndon's unnecessary irritations. Besides, it taught me a knowledge and a love of the district, whose depths I had never really plumbed before. I have always been more interested in politics since then."

The President says of that crisis in their lives: "Bird moved out of our apartment and rented it furnished to help with family finances. She took an apartment way out in Virginia with Nellie Connally [wife of the present Governor of Texas, who was wounded during the assassination of President Kennedy], so they could save money. Bird ran my office so well that I was re-elected. The tenth district would happily have elected her over me, if she had run."

That experience completed the metamorphosis of Lady Bird Johnson from a diffident young wife into a mature woman. The cocoon of her sheltered girlhood had burst, and she now began to regard the world of business and politics as a personal challenge. Many years later, when in a public-speaking class she was assigned the topic, "The Year of Decision," it was of that first wartime year that she spoke.

Representative Johnson returned to Congress in August of 1942, and soon thereafter the Johnsons heard that a small radio station in Austin was for sale. Investigating, they learned that KTBC was without a nighttime franchise or network connection, had only 250 watts of power, 9 employees, and an indebtedness to nearly every bank in town.

Because Lyndon had served as editor of his college paper and Lady Bird had a journalism degree, the Johnsons had long dreamed of owning a newspaper, but they could not afford to buy one. Now they began to consider the radio station as a possible substitute. Bird's father had remarried and was anxious to pay her the remainder of her mother's inheritance, which he had been profitably investing for her.

The remaining cash amount, above the several thousand acres of Alabama farmland, came to twenty-one thousand dollars, which she used to acquire the station and its obligations. The following February the Federal Communications Commission granted approval for the sale, and Bird went to Austin to investigate KTBC's problems. She found that they were legion. Many of the bad debts listed on the debit side were actually management errors. The previous owners, after selling five advertising spots a week to a company, would run the advertisement a sixth time and try to collect for the bonus.

It soon became obvious that Bird would need a new manager for the station. While she was interviewing applicants, she was also reading every contract from the big print through the small, trying to evaluate the staff that she had inherited and seeking to develop and enlarge the business.

Except for an occasional flight to Washington, she remained seven months in Austin, until the station for the first time showed a profit in operations—eighteen dollars. She then returned to the capital, feeling as proud of her purchase as if she had just won an election on her own. She would not, however, have dreamed that in two decades the debt-ridden radio station and the affiliates bought with its profits would burgeon into a multimillion-dollar radio-television property with more than a hundred employees.

The First Lady remembers those wartime years as "a homemaking juggling act." She was now determined to make their apartment a "quiet oasis" for Lyndon, but like every other housewife she seemed to spend half of her day queuing up at grocery and meat counters for supplies.

Once they were entertaining at dinner when she discovered that they had neither butter nor points to buy any. Conquering her innate timidity, she telephoned the guests to see who could spare some. With a merry laugh she recalls that as the wife of a Supreme Court Justice arrived that evening, she slipped a pound of butter from under her shawl.

Bird was still as wide-eyed about the wonders of Washington as she had been on her first trip. Friends and newcomers poured into Washington, and she tirelessly made the sightseeing rounds with them, from Mount Vernon to the Washington Monument. Lyndon was working long hours at the Capitol, and there was little money or time for other diversion.

The day came when Bird, Nellie Connally, and Ann Worley, wife of Congressman Eugene Worley of Texas, decided to stage a minor revolt. In their sightseeing rounds the three Southern women had gazed wistfully at the ice skaters in an arena on Wisconsin Avenue. Skimping on their household money, they put aside six dollars each to buy a pair of skates, and had experienced several jarring falls before they confessed the extravagance to their husbands. To this day, when the three couples get together the men turn to their wives and say, "By the way, whatever happened to those skates? Have you won any contests yet?"

Lyndon, like most husbands, had no sooner married the girl whom he considered perfection than he began trying to make her over into a new mold. He urged Bird to dress more fashionably and started selecting her wardrobe for her. To please him, she cut her hair, and switched from tailored, golfing dresses to bold reds and yellows that hugged her figure. She liked comfortable low-heeled shoes with straps, but Lyndon put her into spike-heeled pumps. "I don't like muley-lookin' things," he would drawl.

During their first five years in Congress, the Johnsons lived in ten different apartments, moving back and forth between Washington and Austin as the sessions adjourned and reconvened. Aunt Effie was spending nearly half of her time with them, and the strain of packing and unpacking became so great that Bird yearned for a place of her own.

"The central theme of my heart's desire was a house," the First Lady reminisces smilingly. "Aunt Effie understood this, so she offered to help with the purchase, and she made the largest part of the payment. Then she just wrote in her will that this was an advance on what she planned to leave me."

Lady Bird excitedly went out in quest of her dream house, and finally found it on a quiet street in the northwest section of Washington. It was a two-story brick colonial, with a screened verandah in the rear. She rushed home, stars in her eyes, to tell Lyndon about it, and found him talking politics as usual with his administrative assistant, John Connally.

When Bird had rapturously finished her description, Lyndon resumed his conversation with Connally without a word. The usually sweet-tempered Bird was furious! For once in her life she sizzled, and in a strained tone exclaimed: "I want that house! Every woman wants a home of her own, and all that I have to look forward to is the next election!"

With that, she stormed from the room. Lyndon, stunned by such unusual behavior on the part of his normally acquiescent wife, scratched his head and asked Connally what he thought he should do.

"I'd buy the house," his aide replied.

And Lyndon did, but not until he had bargained down the price by another two thousand dollars. By that time, he may even have thought the whole thing was his own idea.

After cramped apartment living the eight-room abode seemed like a palace, but eighteen years later, when Lyndon ran for Vice-president, Bird was to say of it: "We've parlayed this very simple little John Citizen home as far as it will go. We're bursting at the seams. We need more closet space for our daughters' starched petticoats, and if Lyndon is elected I'll need more than one long evening dress a year, which is all I've been buying until now."

Having a house of their own did not solve the moving problems for Representative and Mrs. Lyndon B. Johnson in the decade of the forties. They still lived so frugally that whenever Congress prepared to adjourn in midsummer, Bird began looking for a renter. Two weeks of every year were spent in a frenzy of sorting, packing, shipping, unpacking, and straightening. She had to make decisions, decisions, decisions. What should she do with the tons of books and *Congressional Records* that a man in public life accumulates? What should she leave out for the renters, and what should be locked up or stored? What should she take to Texas that they would be sure to need before January?

The house *had* to be rented. Like most other Congressional couples, they needed the income from that to pay for living quarters back in the district. The emptying of closets, drawers, and desks twice a year became such a bugaboo that Bird sighed to friends: "Sometimes I think my idea of being rich would be not having to rent the house."

Bird, who longed for children, had suffered several miscarriages, but after ten years of marriage a baby girl was born. Lyndon proudly named her Lynda Bird for both of them, and jubilantly awakened every member of his Congressional staff in the middle of the night to telephone the glad tidings.

Recently, in talking about his wife's courage, the President said: "Bird waited ten years to have a baby, and has lost four children through miscarriages. She is never a person who will admit her own pain. I remember one time she was running a high temperature, but she insisted that it was all right for me to go to the office. The minute that I left the room she called the doctor. She was bleeding, and in terrific pain with a tubular pregnancy, but she just won't admit pain, or ask for mercy. If she has any fault, this is it."

That pregnancy, which nearly cost her life, occurred when Lynda Bird was two years old. Aunt Effie was in a sanitarium in Birmingham, Alabama, and some months later Bird received a call that the dear old lady was failing rapidly. She went immediately to Birmingham and spent several weeks with Aunt Effie there, reading and talking to her.

"Almost all of the other kinfolks came from time to time," the First Lady recalls, "and when we went out for meals together we would talk about old times. It was a mixture of sadness, reminiscences, and sweetness. I was feeling pretty wretched at the time, and had a pretty good idea of what was the matter. After Aunt Effie rallied and I finally returned to Washington, a doctor confirmed that I was pregnant again."

Shortly thereafter, in January of 1947, Aunt Effie died. A liver ailment had hastened the end, and Bird had ached to be with her, but because of the danger from the tubular pregnancy a year before, the physicians forbade this journey. Bird grieved deeply for the beloved little old lady, but her happiness returned when Lucy Baines arrived safely on July second. Now they were four—all with the same initials—and as Lyndon said: "It's cheaper this way, because we can all use the same luggage."

The first campaign in which Lady Bird actively participated was the hardest fought of Lyndon's political career. He had been winning re-election to the House with monotonous regularity, despite an occasional opponent, but in 1948, he decided to make a second try for the Senate. In Governor Coke Stevenson he faced a formidable opponent, who had survived thirty years of politics without defeat.

Stevenson led in the Democratic primary by a large margin, but since he lacked a majority of the votes a runoff was necessary between him and Lyndon, who had placed second. Of his wife's efforts in his behalf, the President pridefully recalls: "Bird set about to organize the women. She hated to fly. It always made her sick, but she got busy and flew all over the state. The night before the election, she was riding in a car that overturned twice. She got out of the mud, stood in a reception line in a dress borrowed from her hostess, and then joined me in San Antonio to make a speech. She didn't even tell me about that accident, for fear it'd worry me.

"When we got back to the hotel around midnight, I told her we'd better get to bed, but she said she had to go on to Austin that night to do some last-minute campaigning in the morning. As she changed for the trip, I saw those big bruises, and she had to confess. But she went right on to Austin and got on the telephone with Mother and my sisters, and they called everyone in the Austin phone book on my behalf. We carried Austin three-to-one, thanks to that, but we barely carried the state by eighty-seven votes."

Lady Bird views that now historic campaign as "a sort of endurance contest of the spirit." They had thought they were going to win the primary, "but we were overwhelmingly, vastly, horribly behind by a hundred thousand votes." Even the runoff looked hopeless, "but at least I wanted to narrow that margin, not only for Lyndon, but for the sake of those folks who had shoveled so much love and sweat and time and money into the campaign."

Mrs. Max Brooks, a close friend, and Bird set up an organization to woo volunteers. Mrs. Brooks made lists of all the clubwomen she knew in the state, and Bird canvassed everyone she or Lyndon could recall from school and college days, as well as the people he had helped while with the National Youth Administration.

Bird found the courage to ask the wives and mothers to pitch into the campaign, and as the Johnsons toured from town to town, the women held little gatherings for neighbors in their homes. Wherever they went, from Beeville to

Seguin to Marshall and Jefferson, Lyndon and Lady Bird endlessly shook hands with these kindly small-town "folks" who had assembled to meet them. At first, Bird found it acutely embarrassing to praise her own husband to other women, but after a while she realized that "these people are just like me, so I had no reason to be scared." On election day after the automobile accident, she was even able to call strangers "right down the line" in the Austin telephone book.

The eighty-seven-vote margin was so close that legal battles continued from late August until January, when Lyndon at last was sworn in as a Senator. Now his grandfather's prophecy had come to pass, but his new colleagues nicknamed him "Landslide Lyndon." Recalling that tense period before her husband was finally seated as a Senator, the First Lady winces and says: "It must have been something like the feeling that presses in on a person in a wartime concentration camp under prolonged questioning."

As usual, however, Bird can find a silver lining for the experience. "What pleased me most," she muses, "was seeing that Lyndon was the calmest one in that group of capable, tough, hardy lawyers who were working with him and advising him. He was calm and level-headed in a crisis that was enough to make anybody jump out of his skin."

Now that Lyndon was assured of his job for six years, Bird zestfully threw herself into the joyous task of redecorating their eight-room house. Her sudden marriage fourteen years before had deprived her of restoring the family mansion in East Texas, but now she gave full range to her frustrated talents as an amateur decorator. Unfortunately, Lyndon wanted to help, too.

Although the Senator was frequently working eighteen-hour days at the Capitol, he could not resist dabbling in Bird's province. After a few disasters she learned that the discreet way to let her husband select furniture and fabrics was to show him three samples, any one of which she could live with.

"That," she confided to friends, "is the safest way to ensure that we both like them."

Lyndon gave her free rein in paying the household bills, keeping the tax records, and signing checks for her radio-TV station. This detail work would have bored him as much as reading novels or seeing motion-picture shows. Bird's favorite indulgence has always been reading in bed —she regards it as "sort of like eating candy"—and before dropping off to sleep in their double bed, she would often interrupt Lyndon's perusal of the *Congressional Record* to read him something which she felt that he should know.

With the assistance of Genevieve Hendricks, a decorator friend, Bird furnished the house in restful shades of green and beige, but the master bedroom was done in yellow, "because Lyndon thinks it's such a cheerful color for starting the day."

As a Senatorial couple the Johnsons were immediately swept into the upper strata of Washington official society. Sometimes they dined at the embassies, where the country-bred girl from Texas gloried in the sight of sari-clad women with diamonds in their noses and men with ostrich-plumed turbans and red sashes. It was, she decided, "something like frosting on a cake."

Bird frankly liked the glittering parties, and she suspected that Lyndon did, too, although he managed to get out of going whenever he could by pleading that he was too busy. Reminiscing about those early struggling years in the Senate, the First Lady smiles and says: "When he occasionally did break away from work long enough to go to a party, I noticed that Lyndon was usually the hardest one to persuade to leave, after being the hardest one to get there."

Chapter
5

LYNDON BAINES JOHNSON was obviously going places in a hurry. In those days it was unusual for a freshman Senator to receive a major committee assignment of his choice, but this man of destiny won a coveted seat on the Armed Services Committee. Throwing his tremendous energy into the work, he began performing yeoman service for Chairman Richard Russell, just as he had for Chairman Carl Vinson on the House Naval Affairs Committee in the New Deal days.

The purposeful Texan had been a big man in the House. His father's close friend, Sam Rayburn, was the Speaker, and Lyndon himself was on a first-name basis with more Congressmen and their secretaries than most of his senior colleagues. Being the kind of man that he is, the extroverted new Senator found it difficult to adhere to the unwritten rule that freshmen members should be seen but not heard.

He spent the time restlessly learning everything that he could about Senate tradition, and studied the characteristics of the leaders in the so-called upper chamber. Thanks to his wartime experience and ten-year tenure on the House military committee, he became increasingly alarmed by President Harry S. Truman's postwar "whittling away" of our defensive strength.

He could not hold his tongue any longer, and early in 1950 he made an important speech calling for a penetrating review of American foreign and military policy. Four months later, at the outbreak of war in Korea, he praised the President's prompt action in sending troops to defend the strategic peninsula against the Communists, but more importantly, he introduced a resolution to establish a Preparedness Investigating Subcommittee of the Senate Armed Services Committee. The Senate promptly passed the resolution, and although it was virtually unprecedented for a freshman Senator to receive such an accolade, Lyndon was designated its chairman.

Now he was busier than ever, and if Bird wanted to catch a glimpse of her long-legged husband she had to attend the hearings. It was a momentous task that Lyndon had undertaken, but the Subcommittee eventually saved taxpayers several billion dollars, and LBJ proved such a master of cajolery and persuasion that all forty-six of the committee reports were unanimous.

Bird, now a member of the Senate Ladies' Red Cross unit, wrapped bandages every Tuesday while some of the women knitted for veterans' hospital patients. Between times she ran her rapidly expanding business interests, and often served as both mother and father to their two little girls.

Lucy was now three and pining for a dog. Lady Bird was not. Thirteen years later, seated in the upstairs family quarters at the White House, Bird and Lucy chuckled together over that long ago incident. Asked about their most vivid recollections of the new President as a family man, Bird began the narrative like this: "Our Lucy Baines, when she was three years old, began to ask for a dog. I had any number of reasons for not wanting one. In the first place, after years of yearning for them I had just acquired some beautiful carpets of which I was very proud; and second, we were moving back and forth between Washington and Austin each year. I had had the experience of traveling with a cat, and I didn't want to repeat it with a dog, so I just sorta delayed.

"I didn't know how to go about finding a dog. I couldn't find the right kind of a dog. You know—all the reasons you think of for not doing the things you don't want to do. Then one night, when a blizzard was raging outside, Lyndon came home with a big smile, a heavy overcoat, and a big box in his arms. He put the box down on the living-room rug and called Lucy Baines to come and look.

"Lucy got down and peered into the box, and when she raised her face, I have never seen such a beatific expression on any angel. In the box was a beagle, age six weeks, and as cute and lively as he could be. He came to be the joy of the whole family, but he was more especially Lucy Baines' dog, except for the period when Lyndon had his heart attack, and then he devoted himself entirely to Lyndon."

At this point Lucy excitedly took over the story, saying·

[43]

"Mother's only reaction when I opened that box and my eyes nearly popped out of my head was to groan, 'Oh, my rugs!' Daddy had gone in the blizzard clear down into Virginia and finally found him at some kennel near Middleburg."

They named him, of course, Little Beagle Johnson, so that his initials would match those of the rest of the family.

The thriving LBJ ranch near Johnson City, Texas, is a thing of beauty now, but the same could not be said for it in the fall of 1951. The Johnsons and Senator and Mrs. Stuart Symington flew to Texas one weekend on a pleasure trip—or so Bird thought. It was Evie Symington's first introduction to the Lone Star State. The two couples were house guests of their wealthy mutual friends, the Wesley W. Wests.

From the Wests' ranch they all flew to the Dallas stadium for a football game in their host's private plane, and Evie was frankly dazzled by such king-sized operations. "I couldn't get over those beautiful Texas women in their gorgeous hats and frocks, and the men in their expensive gabardine suits, as they stepped from their private planes at the stadium," Evie recalls. "The planes were lined up like a fleet of cars, but the owners were carrying thermos bottles and rugs, just as if they had arrived by family sedan.

"We visited many luxurious ranches that weekend, and it was like another world to me. Then we drove over to the ranch that Lyndon wanted to show us. There was no bridge, so we had to ford the stream to reach the little stone house on the place. Bird seemed appalled, and frankly I shared her feeling, but Lyndon looked at the run-down old place and exclaimed excitedly: 'Let's buy it!' The ranch had

[44]

belonged to his grandparents, but his eighty-year old aunt owned it then."

After Bird became First Lady, I asked if she could recall her reaction at the thought of buying it. Bursting into laughter, she exclaimed: "Certainly I remember my reaction to it. It was one of complete withdrawal. I thought, 'Oh, my Lord, no!' We had just gotten the house in Washington a short while before, and I did so love to be there. I knew the old stone ranchhouse would take *so* much work to fix up. I could hardly bear the thought of it!"

As usual, however, Bird subjugated her own desires to those of her husband. Discussing it years later in the White House, she said: "After I came to sense how completely Lyndon was immersed in the rocks and hills and live oaks of this, his own native land, and how much strength he drew from it, I gradually began to get wrapped up in it myself. I always have loved living on the land. It was just that I had grown up on such a completely different sort of land."

They bought the four-hundred-acre ranch, naturally, and with her customary efficiency Lady Bird plunged energetically into the task of restoring, adding onto, and redecorating the main ranchhouse. The front of the home place faces the Pedernales River, which they dammed, and as Bird stood on the verandah watching sheep grazing down to the water's edge, it began to remind her of a biblical scene. The stone section of the house was more than a hundred years old, and with the white wings and gables added through the years, the total effect suggested to her a Charles Addams' haunted house. The children, however, adored it.

When a friend asked young Lynda Bird whether she

liked the ranch, the schoolgirl replied exuberantly, "Like it? That's like asking whether a cow likes her calf."

The First Lady says of it: "The ranch is Lyndon's spiritual home, where he derives strength and sustenance, so I have a tenderness for it. His roots are there for three generations."

Neighboring ranchers came to the housewarming, bringing not only pies and cakes and preserves but clippings of pink-flowering Queen Anne's wreath to plant along the fences. Lady Bird also had the field hands plant acres of bluebonnets, which are native to that desert-like area of Texas, with its cactus and caliche, and she eventually grew to love the eroded, chalky limestone hills of their "heart's home."

The Johnsons had previously bought an entire household of furniture for a few hundred dollars from an elderly woman in Washington, and they shipped this to the ranch. Bird chose mellow interior colors that blended with the native landscape, and took care to preserve all traces of her beloved mother-in-law, including a lilac "sweetheart" quilt which the elder Mrs. Johnson had made for her as a Christmas present.

The ranch has never paid for itself, in part because of LBJ's expansive hospitality, so despite Bird's growing affluence, she continued to watch the pennies in Washington. For ten years they had had a cook, the faithful Zephyr Wright, who now presides over the family kitchen in the White House, but it was Bird who had to soothe the ruffled feelings when Lyndon sometimes wanted dinner at midnight or brought constituents home unannounced for a meal.

They entertained occasionally with informal buffet suppers, and guests filed down the narrow basement steps to the recreation room to help themselves to Zephyr's famed chili con carni, homemade breads, and fried chicken. They would eat at gaily bedecked tables set up in the basement, and then return to the pale green drawing room for hours of political talk.

Largely through the influence of Senator Richard Russell of Georgia, the powerful Southerner whom Lyndon had taken pains to cultivate and serve, LBJ was elected Democratic whip in 1951, although he had held his Senate seat for only two years. When Senator Ernest McFarland was defeated for re-election the next year by Republican Senator Barry Goldwater, first-termer Lyndon Johnson became the Minority Leader.

Republicans were then in control of Congress for the first time since Herbert Hoover's day, thanks to the landslide victory of President Dwight D. Eisenhower; but in the off-year Congressional elections of 1954, Democrats regained control of Capitol Hill. Lyndon, having won re-election that year, now became, at forty-six, the youngest Senate Majority Leader in American history. Even his far-sighted granddaddy had not envisioned such a family triumph as this!

Because of the campaigning and the speech-making trips, Bird and Lyndon frequently had to leave their two little girls behind with a nursemaid. Sometimes devoted members of Lyndon's staff—Mary Rather or Willie Day Taylor—also slept at the house to oversee the lively children. Miss Rather was on tap once while both Lynda and Lucy had the mumps, and another time when Lynda, rushing at full speed into the living room to show her the first cherry pie she had ever baked, tripped on a rug and fell. The cherry pie landed upside down in Miss Rather's lap.

Miss Rather says of the girls: "They were normal, exuberant children full of love and affection, very hospitable and out-going with friends and never shy even with strangers. Lady Bird guided their manners, supervised their friends, and taught them the independence and self-confidence that her father's early training had instilled in her.

"Lynda and Lucy were not told that children are to be seen and not heard. They were never kept upstairs out of sight, even at dinner parties. They usually had their dinner early, but were always presented to guests and allowed to converse with them for awhile. Although Speaker Rayburn was an elderly bachelor, he had a winning way with little girls and they adored him. He always came to their birthday parties, and they would climb on his lap to dispense kisses and secrets.

"The Johnsons were always affectionate and demonstrative. Their father would arrive home shouting for kisses, and Lynda and Lucy would bound into his arms to shower them upon him. They would 'save sugar behind their ears' all day, and with much laughter he would 'gobble it up' when he hugged them."

Lucy was always more domestically inclined than Lynda. Once, when a guest spilled something on the carpeting, little Lucy fled to the kitchen and returned with a wet cloth to mop the spot.

Every Sunday morning a large special delivery envelope would arrive from Station KTBC in Austin. Even in her pre-school days Lucy would watch for the mailman, and carry the parcel upstairs to Lady Bird, saying importantly: "This is Mother's business."

Lady Bird recalls one hilarious time when Lynda Bird had a "very mild childhood disease called impetigo," while Bird was on business at KTBC in Austin. She says: "I simply could not come back because matters were crucial, but Lyndon! You would have thought that Lynda Bird had cancer, the way Lyndon behaved! He called Mrs. Albert Thomas [wife of the Representative from Houston], who got the doctor, and came over and helped him out. Lyndon since then has considered himself and Lera Thomas veritable lifesavers, because that skin eruption didn't finish her."

The tempo of life for Lady Bird and Lyndon had stepped up to such a fever pitch that neither of them had as much time as they would have liked for their high-spirited daughters, who began referring to themselves as de-privileged children. This saddened Bird, who says: "Naturally they crave more of our companionship and attention, but I have tried to impress on them that their father's job is important. I assure them, however, that such importance doesn't rub off on them. Self-importance is nuts, I tell them; self-responsibility is the thing to aspire to."

Lady Bird, having been a motherless child, showered her two little girls with affection. She called them "loved one" and "cupcake," and never parted from them without saying gently, "Remember, you are loved."

Looking back at those years from the vantage point of the White House, the First Lady says softly: "We were greatly blessed by having a nursemaid, who was also a friend, to stay with the children. Since Lucy was two, we have had Helen Williams with us. She was so very affectionate with the children, and had the household so well organized, that I didn't feel too bad about leaving them occasionally."

The children were taught their manners, too. One day, when the Senator took Lucy Baines along to his office, the little four-year-old climbed up on Willie Day Taylor's lap and lisped: "Mummy says you can't go any place 'les you're invited, but if you wuz to 'vite me, I could spend the weekend with you."

Willie had herself a house guest until Sunday.

Ann Worley laughingly recalls the time that Bird returned home to find the house full of Lynda Bird's seven-year-old playmates. It was nearing the Christmas season, and when she asked Lynda what they were doing, the youngster replied, "Playing Jesus."

The startled Bird then asked what kind of a game that was, and Lynda gravely explained that Sue was playing Mary, Jane was playing Joseph, and Lucy was the Christ Child. Somewhat surprised that Lynda had assigned all the leading roles to others, Bird asked, "What part are you playing?"

"Oh, I'm Roy Rogers," Lynda replied with alacrity.

Lyndon was taking no time from his busy schedule to relax or attend parties. Once, feeling rather diffident about it, Bird went to an embassy dinner-dance without him. Later, as they were undressing for bed, she said plaintively, "Lyndon, I don't see why you can't take some time off for fun now and then. All the other Senators do. Why, Senator Theodore Francis Green asked me to dance twice tonight."

"Senator Green!" her husband bellowed. "Well, what

kept me at work so late tonight was passing his pet bill through the Senate."

Lyndon's pace continued unabated, but something had to snap—and it did. He was a fretting, fidgety leader who found it difficult to sit still. From the gallery, his wife could watch his long-legged stride as he bolted about the Senate floor, buttonholing fellow Democrats who were threatening to defect from his policy line and wooing friendly Republicans.

He had become more powerful than any Senate leader in history, gradually pulling into his own two hands the tight reins of Senate supremacy. Not only did he retain the chairmanships of the Policy and Steering committees—the chief levers of Senate power—but he also held seats on several other committees, including the Appropriations and Armed Services. He drove his colleagues hard and himself even harder.

On Saturday, July 2, 1955, he worked as usual at the Senate, although it was Lucy's eighth birthday. In the morning he held a press conference, and when a reporter tactlessly remarked that it was strange that the majority leader did not seem to know when the immigration bill would come up for a vote, Lyndon blew his top. Always thin-skinned about criticism, he snapped at the newsman.

He lunched with his old friends, Speaker Rayburn and Senator Symington, and they told him that he was working too hard. He would have made no such outburst, they felt, if he were more relaxed. He admitted to them that he was tired, but said that he was going out to the Virginia estate of an old Texas friend, George Brown, to spend the Fourth of July weekend. He believed that he could get some much-needed rest in the open air.

Before starting for the country he rushed out to order one dark blue and one brown suit to replace some worn seersuckers that Lady Bird had been chiding him about. He also dropped by the Mayflower Hotel to call on elderly Senator Walter George, who was not feeling well. Miss Lucy, the Georgia Senator's wife, offered him a drink, but he was too hurried to take it.

Norman Edwards, Lyndon's chauffeur was waiting. As they headed into the rolling Virginia countryside, Lyndon experienced "a closed-in" feeling and asked the driver to turn on the air conditioner. Edwards replied that it was already on all the way and that the car was quite cold.

The inner pressure increased, and Lyndon regretted that he had eaten a cantaloupe at lunch. He recalls that he "belched and felt a little better," but his chest ached as if it carried "a two-hundred-pound weight." By the time they reached the Brown's estate, he was so uncomfortable that he asked the chauffer to wait a while, in the event that he had to return home.

His host gave him some bicarbonate of soda and he lay down, but had difficulty breathing. Senator Clinton P. Anderson who was a member of the cardiac club, thought he recognized the symptoms and persuaded Lyndon to let Brown call a doctor. When the physician had examined his patient, he, too, worried about a heart attack, and the the suffering patient exclaimed, "If you think it might be a heart attack, let's act as though we know it is."

While he waited for the ambulance to take him to Bethesda Naval Hospital near Washington, Lyndon told his friends to call Lady Bird and also Senate Secretary Skeeter Johnston, two of his own assistants, and his personal doctor. He wanted them all to be at the hospital when he arrived. In the ambulance he smoked a cigarette, although the doctor had asked him not to. It was the last one he has smoked.

Bird, who had not expected to join her husband at the Browns until the next day because of Lucy's birthday party, received news of her husband's illness by telephone and rushed to the Naval Hospital. So did Walter Jenkins, Lyndon's long-time executive assistant, and as the Senator was lifted from the stretcher he told Jenkins: "My money clip's in my coat pocket. Give it to Bird. She'll be needing cash right away. If things don't turn out all right, my will is in the safe at the office. Take care of things, Walter."

He reached for his wife's hand and gazed deeply into her concerned and loving face. "Stay with me, Bird," he pleaded, like a small boy, before he went into shock.

Lady Bird moved into an adjoining room at the hospital and remained throughout the six weeks Lyndon stayed there. His doctors had immediately put him on such a stringent diet that his practical wife wondered aloud whether she should cancel the order for his two new suits. The cardiac patient knew perfectly well that she meant they probably would not fit him by the time he was ready to wear them, but with an impish grin he retorted: "We might as well keep the dark blue one, Bird. We'll need that one, either way. . . ." Now they were able to laugh together.

At first, Bird would not leave him even long enough to go out for a meal, but after a week or so, when Judge— former Representative—and Mrs. Eugene Worley called to urge her to go with them to El Chico's restaurant for some Mexican food, the temptation proved irresistible. They called for her at the hospital, and Ann Worley will never forget how determinedly gay and cheerful Bird was that evening. "Everything's goin' to be fine," she said optimistically, as if to convince herself.

Bird converted the adjoining hospital room into a combination bedroom-office, from which she helped Lyndon's staff to handle the business of his office, and worked on her own radio-television interests. Her task was not easy, however, because Lyndon wanted her beside him twenty-four hours a day, and he wanted her to wear bright lipstick—and laugh.

Lynda and Lucy sensed a subtle change in their parents, when they at last came home from the hospital. They seemed closer to each other than ever before, and Lyndon could scarcely bear to have Bird out of his sight. He was as demanding as ever, but Lynda Bird says of the relationship: "Daddy worships Mother. He tells her his problems and seeks her advice. It's just that he doesn't realize that sometimes she might want to weep on *his* shoulder."

To a close friend Bird had observed: "When Lyndon is out of danger, and the crisis is past, I just want to go off alone somewhere and cry."

Considering his flambuoyant temperament, Lyndon was a reasonably good patient at first. A three-pack-a-day cigarette smoker, he cut them out entirely. Under doctors' orders he had gone on a stringent diet, which pared his weight from 225 pounds to 184, and he forced himself to lie quietly for hours at a time. After he had returned home, it required all of Bird's innate tact and resourcefulness to make him continue the same regime. Meticulous in everything that she does, she bought scales and carefully weighed every ounce of his food. She schooled Zephyr in the art of low-calorie cookery, and praised Lyndon end-lessly for his co-operation and willingness.

At first, Lyndon was surprisingly docile; but as the danger receded, he was like a penned lion pacing his cage. Majority Whip Earl Clements had become acting majority leader, but it would have been unlike Lyndon not to try to keep his finger on the pulse of power, even while resting at home.

As soon as Lyndon was able to make the trip to Texas, Dr. Willis Hurst accompanied the Johnsons on their flight to the ranch. The famous heart specialist remained until his patient was well settled and he had briefed local doctors about the case. He then left Lady Bird with minute instructions as to diet and rest, and urged that Lyndon be kept free of visitors, irritations, decisions, or work. This was a sad, still period in Bird's life.

Mary Rather, who spent the fall with them at the ranch, recalls that they retired each evening at nine o'clock and rose at an early hour. The rural mail carrier left the morning papers and mail about six A.M., and Miss Rather would dash across the river to get them from the box. Some mornings they sat under the big live oak tree on the lawn to read them, but at other times LBJ seemed disinterested in the news.

"Whatever Lyndon did, Lady Bird did with him," Miss Rather says. "How she managed to run the house, attend her children, talk to visitors who came uninvited but with good intentions, and still take care of her husband, I sometimes wondered."

Lyndon's constant refrain was, "Where's Lady Bird?"

And she was always near enough at hand to answer for herself, "Here I am, darling."

The threat of another heart attack was ever in their thoughts. They kept digitalis handy for a while, but it did not have to be used. Also hanging over them was the decision Lyndon would soon have to make about whether to resume his position as Senate majority leader. To risk another heart attack by doing so was unthinkable, but so—for LBJ—was the thought of giving up.

Says Mary Rather: "For hours Mr. Johnson would lie in a reclining chair, thinking and dozing, with the beagle dog stretched out on his lap asleep. Finally, he and the dog would stir and walk slowly to the gate and back. The first time that he laughed was when the dozing beagle suddenly deserted him like a streak, in chase of an unsuspecting rabbit. Each day Mr. Johnson walked a little longer, and in time a mile or two, wearing a pedometer which his sister gave him.

"Being completely idle was something Mr. Johnson could not abide for long. Lady Bird, ever agreeable, said not a word as the north side of the yard became a gaping hole, and then a swimming pool; nor when music was piped from the living room to the dining room and out of a tree near the pool. Next came repairs and paint on the home of an elderly relative down the lane. Gradually, we began to take afternoon rides to watch the deer, and think about a possible hunt in November."

Lady Bird and the cook counted calories and learned delicious, non-fattening recipes. Juanita Roberts, a member of Lyndon's office staff who was also a dietitian, planned protein-rich menus which shunned starches, fats, and sugars. The women talked so much about proteins that Lyndon banned the use of the word in his presence, but when he asked Juanita what he could do about the flabby look around his face, which came with the weight loss, she replied bravely, "Proteins."

As his strength and interests gradually returned, Bird occasionally invited three sharp domino players, A. W. Moursund and Melvin Winters of Johnson City and Everett Looney of Austin, to spend the evening. Like everything else that he does, Lyndon played to win, and the heated bouts helped to restore his competitive spirit. The Winters' brought him a walnut rocking chair, and Moursund—later to be named one of the two trustees for Lady Bird's television holdings—drove by nearly every day for a short report on the land, the cattle, and the latest news of Johnson City.

With returning confidence Lady Bird began inviting friends for afternoon swims in which her husband joined. Afterward, they sat around the pool sipping bouillon poured over ice, or lemonade made with sugarless sweeteners.

Lyndon's interest in his work gradually returned, and he would sit at a card table in the living room to handle his mail. Mary Rather worked at the desk, and long telephone cords were strung across the living room so that he could keep in daily communication with Walter Jenkins in Washington and George Reedy at his Austin office.

All of his public appearances had been canceled except one: a Democratic fund-raising dinner sponsored by the twelfth district at Whitney, Texas. Originally scheduled for September, it was postponed after Lyndon's heart attack until November. He and Lady Bird arrived to hear the enthusiastic cheers of 1,500 Texans, who overflowed

[57]

the gymnasium in the little town whose population was only 1,050.

Speaker Sam Rayburn came to the ranch with Adlai Stevenson one moonlit night, and they sat on the lawn talking till past midnight. Little Beagle slept on LBJ's lap, a cow mooed, and the river flowed gently by. At dawn the next morning the yard was full of newspaper and television reporters, and the three men held an impromptu press conference, Lyndon's first since the day of his heart attack.

Other visitors on the political scene began to make the pilgrimage to the ranch: Senators Russell, Symington, Clements, Smathers, and Kerr; Governor Price Daniel; John Connally; Representative Homer Thornberry; and other Texans. Senator George Smathers of Florida had chosen a cool night for his visit, and the next day he confessed that he had spread his overcoat over the bedcovers to keep warm. Bird was embarrassed. She had not thought to tell him that the fancy gadget on his bedside table was the switch for his electric blanket.

Rebekah Johnson, Lyndon's widowed mother, came often from Austin to visit, and occupied a downstairs bedroom so that she would not have to climb the stairs. His brother and sisters came, as did Lady Bird's two brothers, their wives, and her father.

LBJ's office personnel also began to arrive, and Bird seldom knew how many would be there for dinner or how many would spend the night. The one thing that Bird asked of all guests was that they laugh as much as possible and show no visible reaction to Lyndon's loose-fitting clothes. She knew how susceptible he was to the dispositions of those around him.

Everyone co-operated so beautifully that his spirits soon began to soar. When the deer season opened, he awakened Lady Bird and Mary Rather at dawn for their first hunt in a year. He had learned to joke and tease again, and had developed new thoughtfulness. He was a crack shot with a deer rifle, and sometimes when he thought that a guest was not, he would fire simultaneously with his guest. Then he would spend the rest of the day congratulating the visitor for killing a fine buck.

By December he was well enough to take a trip to California with Bird and Mary, to show Lynda and Lucy the charm of Disneyland. It was during that journey, Mary Rather believes, that LBJ determined to resume his duties as majority leader. It was an historic decision, since it was to lead ultimately to the Presidency.

The soothing ministrations of his wife and the restorative magic of the ranch combined to induce an unusually rapid recovery in Lyndon Johnson. A tanned, slimmed-down Lyndon resumed the leadership chair when the Senate reconvened in January. Occasionally he flew down for long weekends at the ranch, but it was not long before he was again maintaining his old breakneck pace at the Capitol. All that his patient wife could do was hope and pray.

Chapter

6

LADY BIRD'S personal fortune was steadily increasing, thanks to the postwar Texas boom and the shrewdness of her investments. The Austin television station, with the only franchise in the capital of the Lone Star State, was expanding rapidly to coincide with the growth of the area; and the parent LBJ Company was acquiring part interests in TV stations at Waco and Bryan, Texas, and Ardmore, Oklahoma.

Bird retained 52.7 percent of the stock, and administered another 30.9 percent for her daughters. She inaugurated a profit-sharing plan for her employees, and permitted certain key executives to buy the remaining outstanding shares. Besides this flourishing business, which required frequent trips to Texas, she was gradually converting her thousands of acres of inherited Alabama cotton land to tree farming.

Lyndon was never too busy to take a personal interest in her wardrobe, and since she was as eager to please him in that respect as any other, she would dutifully take him shopping with her or bring home several dresses so that he could choose. The dashing Senator sometimes made shopping forays on his own, particularly to Neiman-Marcus when he was in Dallas, and would surprise his wife with expensive originals which elegantly set off her trim size-ten figure.

Bird could now hold her own with any other fashionable official wife, but she once said: "I want clothes to serve me, instead of me serving them. I begrudge making a career out of clothes, but Lyndon likes bright colors and dramatic styles that do the most for one's figure, and I try to please him. I've really tried to learn the art of clothes, because you don't sell for what you're worth unless you look well."

Lyndon was one of those fortunate men whose mother and wife were devoted to each other. His father, Sam Ealy Johnson, lived for only a short time after his son was elected to Congress. Rebekah Baines Johnson had never cared for ranch life, and after her husband's death, Lyndon and Bird selected a house for her in Austin.

Speaking of her mother-in-law, who died in 1957, the First Lady declared: "She was the sort of person that I truly enjoyed being with. If I had an extra hour in Austin before I had to catch a plane or train to Washington, and I would think of the many friends I could call, I would decide that I'd rather spend it with Mrs. Johnson. I'd go to see her, and we would sit and talk about books, about household decorating, and family. We just had the good fortune to be friends, which is much better than loving one's in-laws, I think.

"As long as her husband lived, she had no interest except in him and her family, but when he died and the children were raised, her natural and very great intelligence began to grow again, and she followed her girlhood interest in Early American pressed glass, and in genealogy, and in reading lots and lots of books. She would come to Washington to visit Lyndon, and we would have the most delightful trips down into little towns in Virginia to visit courthouses, graveyards, and historical associations, looking up genealogical data."

The President smilingly adds that his mother "used to keep me busy providing her with secretaries to type up all those genealogical records."

The elder Mrs. Johnson accompanied her son and daughter-in-law to the Democratic Convention in 1956. "It was sort of a 'last hurrah' for her," Bird says nostalgically. "After we came back to Washington, she mentioned for the first time some nodules on her arms and said they had been there for quite a little while. It was hard to get her to go to the doctor. We practically had to rope and tie her to make her go. The prognosis was not good. She had cancer of the lymph glands, but the doctor said she might be around for a long, long time. For that much we were grateful."

Lady Bird gazed out of the window at the Washington Monument for a moment, and then continued: "Some very nice things happened during that time. My little Lucy Baines was never very close to her grandmother, but for some reason she began—intentionally and sort of intuitively—to get closer to her. Lynda, Lyndon, and I were spending the same amount of time with Mrs. Johnson that we always had, but Lucy Baines always managed to be around her a little more." A tender light infused her brown eyes as she added: "Mrs. Johnson was the sort of person who always picked out the inscriptions to go on family tombstones, and I love the one she had carved on her husband's tombstone: 'Of purest gold from the Master's hand, a man who loved his fellow man.' Unfortunately, she didn't pick one out for herself."

Christmas holidays were usually spent at the LBJ ranch, and although Lynda and Lucy loved its splendid isolation, Lynda was reaching the age when teenage parties also held enchantment. The year that she was sixteen, she went to visit Mary Rather in Hillsboro, Texas, for a few days during the Yuletide season. The long-time family friend exclaimed enthusiastically at the "new" Lynda.

"She had lost her earlier chubbiness," Miss Rather recalls. "She was slender and stunning, with a perfectly shaped face, lovely eyes, dimples, a clear complexion and slim figure. At mealtimes she ate almost nothing and when I urged her, she said that if she gained a single pound her clothes would be too tight."

Since she was attending numerous parties, Miss Rather assumed that her youthful guest was probably spoiling her appetite with party snacks. However, after a couple of days Lady Bird telephoned from the ranch to ask, "Lynda, do you have my red dress?"

"Yes, Mother, I wore it up here," Lynda replied.

"Well, Lynda, where is my beige sweater and skirt?" Bird continued.

"I have it on, Mother."

"And my pink wool?"

"I brought that too, Mother."

"Lynda, do you realize that you have everything I

brought with me from Washington?" Lady Bird exclaimed. "I have twenty guests coming this afternoon, and I haven't anything to wear. I believe you have taken everything."

After Lynda had pensively returned the phone to the hook, she asked Mary Rather if there was any meatloaf left from lunch. Her hostess hastened to the kitchen, and Lynda decided that she would also like some mashed potatoes, black-eyed peas and a glass of milk.

"I probably won't get to wear Mother's clothes anymore anyway, after I go home tomorrow," she grinned, "so I might as well eat."

Lady Bird, because of her husband's powerful position in government, was frequently asked to speak at women's functions. "I've just come to say howdy," she would say, while her knees trembled. But a small revolt against her own shyness was beginning to churn within her. At a fortuitous time in 1959, she received a telephone call from a long-time friend, Mrs. Dale Miller, whose husband represented several Texas organizations in Washington. "Scooter" Miller reported that Mrs. Hester Provenson was about to start a new Capital Speakers' Club series, and she suggested that they both enroll.

Bird began the class somewhat reluctantly, but soon was throwing herself into it as wholeheartedly as she does into any project that she undertakes. Alone, she practiced her little speeches endlessly before a mirror, and then she would telephone "Scooter" to come over and offer criticism.

The majority leader's wife outranked all others in the class, which was composed principally of women from the foreign diplomatic corps, but she was as anxious to please as any of them. Each was assigned a topic on which to address the class, and although some of the women strove to be witty, or to spoof the subject, Bird's dissertations were invariably serious and earnest.

Explaining why she had agreed to take the course, she says quaintly: "I got real annoyed with myself for being so shy and quiet, and never having anything to say when asked to speak. I took the course, and it turned out to be one of the most delightful, expanding experiences I've ever had. Since then I've talked to a Texas music club about music in Washington, and to another about what it's like to help your husband in business, to say nothing of all the campaign speeches."

To her own surprise she discovered that she enjoyed speech-making. Careful never to interfere in her husband's department, she would avoid political subjects by explaining modestly: "I'm not well enough versed in the pros and cons of that." But with her new-found platform poise, she could add: "Not that I don't think I could learn it, if I really applied myself."

The experience was to prove invaluable the following year, when her husband was running for Vice-president on the Democratic ticket with John F. Kennedy, whose wife had to stay on the sidelines because of her pregnancy. Bird could certainly not have foreseen, while practicing her class assignments before a mirror, that she would soon be called upon to travel thirty-five thousand miles throughout most of the country, addressing hundreds of women's rallies.

Shortly after Bird completed her public-speaking course, Elizabeth Carpenter, a close friend and Texas newspaperwoman who covered political Washington, persuaded her to hold a press conference. Attendance was restricted to women reporters, who were also invited to have refreshments afterward. The evening had been selected with care, to insure that the majority leader would be occupied elsewhere at a National Press Club stag dinner. Bird's self-assurance had not yet reached the stage where she was willing to perform before her husband's critical eye.

A dozen women went to the Johnson's house that evening at the appointed hour. They chatted in easy informality for a time, until Lady Bird relaxed enough to begin. Then the questions began to fly. Lyndon Baines Johnson was already regarded as a leading contender for the 1960 presidential nomination, and they were interested to learn his wife's reactions.

The hostess was fielding questions with reasonably unruffled calm, when suddenly the front door swung open and her rangy husband loomed in the doorway. Another man might have slipped quietly upstairs, but not Lyndon Johnson of Texas. Tossing a grin at his disconcerted wife, the extroverted politician gave each lady a bear hug or a kiss on the cheek, while confessing that he had pulled a fast one on male members of the press. As soon as they dimmed the lights for the entertainment portion of their program, he had slipped out a side door. He was not about to miss Bird's first press conference.

Unlimbering his long legs on the living-room rug, he leaned against a chair and took over his wife's conference. Twelve-year-old Lucy Baines, delighted that the evening was turning into a family party, sprawled on the floor beside him. Not to be outdone, "Little Beagle Johnson," the dog who shared the family initials, bounded into the room and licked at LBJ's shoes.

The Senator's monologue was fascinating, as always, but

when he announced that he was "just talkin' off the record," the reporters laughingly prodded him to leave the room, so that his wife's on-the-record conference could proceed.

Lyndon amiably ambled upstairs, but in a few minutes, drawn like a moth to the flame, he returned to share the spotlight. This time he was reasonably mute for a few minutes, but whenever Bird answered queries he would invariably amplify her remarks. Asked about her automobile smash-up on election eve in Texas a few years before, she had barely begun to relate how she had hitchhiked into town to attend the rally for Lyndon when he took over.

"And do you know," he drawled, "that she didn't tell me anything about that accident for fear it'd worry me?" He then supplied the full details. As he finished, he beamed proudly at his petite wife, and a warm glow suffused her cheeks. Far from being upset by her husband's unexpected take-over of her conference, she was obviously floating on cloud nine. His incredible unpredictability had long since ceased to disturb Lady Bird, but she once confided: "Lyndon is a great hand at saying what he wants, and then expecting me to implement it. He wants music in every room, so I installed it. Once he wanted a new lawn for a party in three weeks—something almost impossible to achieve in the fall—but he got it."

As the election year of 1960 approached, the Johnsons were often in the spotlight. The Democratic race was wide open, since no single candidate stood out as the obvious choice. Senators John F. Kennedy, Hubert Humphrey, and Stuart Symington were patently interested, as was Lyndon; and Jack Kennedy told a newspaper friend: "I know all

[67]

the other candidates pretty well, and I frankly think I'm
as able to handle the Presidency as any of them, or abler—
all except Lyndon, and he hasn't got a chance."

Because he was a Southerner by birth and tradition, LBJ
knew that he had three counts against him. The liberal
Northern faction nearly always controls the Democratic
presidential choice. For this reason, he began telling newsmen that his part of Texas was really "the West"—which
it does more nearly resemble—and that as a Westerner his
interests were more attuned to the Rocky Mountain and
Pacific Coast states than to the regional Southland.

His big Stetson had not yet sailed into the presidential
ring, however, and after Senators Kennedy and Humphrey
had battled it out in the Wisconsin and West Virginia
primaries, and Stuart Symington had belatedly come into
the race, Johnson backers were still restlessly waiting for
the other shoe to drop.

Majority leader Johnson was acting like a candidate, and
talking like a candidate, but as the Congressional session
neared its close, he was still not a declared candidate. At
a Democratic Women's Club dinner the wives of prospec-
tive candidates had been asked to introduce their own husbands. Bird, who by now had almost overcome her reluc-
tance to toot the family horn, presented Lyndon this way:
"Usually at a dinner like this, I listen to someone introduce Lyndon with words of praise and approval, all of
which I underwrite with joy. But I want to introduce him
in a more personal way tonight, as an exciting man to live
with, an exhausting man to keep up with, a man who has
worn well in the twenty-five years we've been together—
and, most important, a man from whom I've learned that

to put all the brains and heart and skill you have into the job of trying to make your government work a little better can be a wonderful life for a man and his wife."

It was typical of Bird, however, that when someone asked if she had ever considered running for public office, she threw up her hands in mock horror and exclaimed: "No, ma'am, I wouldn't want to get up and talk about myself the way you have to do in politics."

Speaker Sam Rayburn and the late Senator Robert Kerr of Oklahoma were putting the heat on their close friend, Lyndon, to get him into the presidential contest without further ado. A few years earlier, when his name had figured less prominently in political speculation, he had said convincingly: "Talk of my being a potential candidate is a lot of foolishness. I have no interest, no ambition in that direction. I'm conscious of my limitations. I think it's fair to say that nobody but my mama ever thought I'd get as far as I am."

Now he was making no such protestations. In 1957 he had steered through the Senate the first civil rights bill since Reconstruction days. Three years later he repeated the near-miracle by beating down a Southern filibuster, to pass another such measure. These actions had alienated some important sections of the South, and Lyndon thought they should have removed the sectional sting of Dixie from his candidacy.

During this tense period in the spring of 1960, while her husband was playing a waiting game, Bird granted occasional press interviews. She limited herself to wifely topics, but averred that she liked to campaign with Lyndon. "I find it interesting and exhilarating," she said diplomatically. "I learn a lot. I feel it's important for me to go along. I think people can assess a man better when they know what kind of wife and family he has. They are interested in the total man. I can be helpful to him on trips, too, by ordering breakfast in the room and making sure there's saccharin for his coffee. I try to remind him of his diet without being obnoxious. I try to draw the line at nagging." Less than a week before the nominating convention was called to order in Los Angeles, Johnson formally announced his candidacy for the presidency. In doing so, he took an oblique dig at the three Senators already running hard for the number one spot, by telling newsmen: "I couldn't announce earlier, because somebody had to tend the store. Those who have engaged in active campaigns have missed hundreds of Senate votes."

Bird again found herself in the eye of the political hurricane, and in answer to questions she confirmed that Lyndon frequently consulted her on important speeches before he made them. "He's kind enough or flattering enough to value my judgment," she said frankly. "I'm likely to have the same basic sort of reaction that many of his constituents would. Lyndon is quite capable of learning from and following the directions of anybody he thinks is wise and knowledgeable, and to a little extent he thinks that I am."

Lady Bird and their two daughters accompanied Lyndon to the Democratic Convention. By now his doctors had given him a clean bill of health. His electrocardiograph record was completely normal and he frequently pulled it out of his pocket to show friends. He had taken no anticoagulants since he left the hospital five years before, nor any digitalis or other heart medicines. Although Lyndon had been fond of telling people that he'd had "as bad a heart attack as a man could undergo and survive," the cardiogram now showed no evidence of heart damage.

Senator George Smathers, the handsome young Florida Solon who had served as an usher at Jack Kennedy's wedding and was his closest Senatorial friend, called a press conference on the opening day of the Convention. It was no secret that Smathers was supporting Johnson rather than his Senate buddy, but he went all out when he declared: "If the American people were given a chance to hire the best man they could find for the presidency, who would they hire? Why, Lyndon Johnson, of course. He is by all odds the best qualified man to guide the destiny of America in these times."

Snappy red-white-and-blue costumes had been designed for LBJ's feminine volunteers, who called themselves "Texans for Lyndon," and by the time the Johnson family walked into his headquarters at the Biltmore Hotel, they had done their work well. The tremendous room was so crowded that the jauntily garbed women could scarcely clear an aisle for their towering candidate and his "women folks" to reach center stage.

Lyndon spoke first, flashing his smile and exuding self-confidence, while his backers roared their enthusiastic approval. Lady Bird and Lynda Bird each spoke briefly, and then thirteen-year-old Lucy Baines took her turn at the microphone. Smiling down at the jampacked throng, she delivered herself of a one-sentence political speech that was to become something of a classic in Convention history. "Gosh," she beamed, "I wish I had as many boy friends as there are people in this room."

Her parents nodded adoringly.

Chapter

7

THE SUSPENSE of the next two days proved almost unbearable for Lynda and Lucy, who had inherited their father's volatile nature, but Bird looked as serene and unflustered as always. While she graciously received callers at Johnson headquarters and in their private suite, Lyndon buttonholed delegates and addressed state caucuses.

"There's a whole stable of politicians and legislators in my family background," he once drawled, "but the smartest of them was my daddy. He used to say that if you couldn't come into a room full of people and tell right away who was for you and who was against you, you had no business in politics."

Lyndon had inherited this faculty to a marked degree. He knew that with his late start and Southern stamp, he was unlikely to win the presidential nomination, but he let no prairie grass grow under his feet. Whenever reporters asked whether he would consider the number two spot on the ticket, he emphatically declared that he would not.

Madame Perle Mesta, queen of the Democratic social set, flew to Los Angeles to cover the convention for NBC radio, but served a daily stint at the Johnson hospitality headquarters plugging for "my friend Lyndon." President Truman's former Minister to Luxemburg radiated optimism. Having deserted the Republican party after the Willkie defeat in 1940, she had correctly predicted all presidential victors ever since. This time, she firmly asserted, it would be Lyndon Baines Johnson all the way.

Mrs. Mesta, whose hospitality is legendary, did far more than shake hands with visitors to Johnson headquarters. Opening her ample pocketbook, she also entertained a few thousand people at a breakfast extravaganza in honor of Lyndon and Lady Bird at the plush Cocoanut Grove.

Every delegate to the Democratic Convention received an invitation, and, judging by the massed humanity, most of them must have accepted. While their plates were heaped high with scrambled eggs and country sausage, an orchestra batted out rhythms and pretty actresses table-hopped their way through the crowds.

Conspicuous by his absence was front-running Candidate John Fitzgerald Kennedy. Perle hadn't invited him because she naturally did not want to promote LBJ's most formidable rival. When anyone remarked on his absence, Perle murmured disarmingly, "I'm told that Jack Kennedy isn't a delegate, but Lyndon just happens to head the Texas delegation. This is a party for delegates."

Lyndon assured Perle, as well as newspaper friends, that he would not settle for second place on the ticket. He well knew that another colorful Texan, former Vice-president John Nance Garner of Uvalde, had once said the job "wasn't worth a pitcher of warm spit." Lyndon regarded the Senate majority leadership as one of the two most powerful posts in the nation, and he was "not about to swap my vote for a gavel."

The night that the balloting began, Bird sat with her two daughters in a box at the National Sports Arena, where the Convention was being held. Glimpsing Dale and "Scooter" Miller in the milling throng, she sent an aide to ask them to join her. The wild exuberance of the demonstration for Johnson, after Sam Rayburn had nominated him, was now behind them. The showdown was at hand.

Nine names had been placed in nomination, but two were withdrawn, and three of the others were merely favorite sons, playing a holding operation. The real spotlight centered on front-runners John F. Kennedy and Lyndon B. Johnson, with former standard-bearer Adlai Stevenson and Senator Stuart Symington also figuring in the speculation as possible compromise candidates in the event of a deadlock.

For a time the balloting seesawed between Kennedy and Johnson, while thousands of eyes surveyed the three Johnson women with appraising glances. The young girls sat tall and straight, but Bird was busy with a pencil, marking the count on her unofficial ballot. Soon the steam roller for Kennedy began to pull away, and by the time the roll call reached Wyoming, the Massachusetts Senator had 750 of the 761 votes required for nomination.

The fifteen votes of Wyoming put him over the top on the first ballot, and while the great arena rocked with wild acclaim for the new Democratic standard-bearer, Lucy Baines burst into violent tears.

Lyndon had placed second, with 409 votes, and for the second time in his life had lost the political prize that he sought. Lady Bird, masking her own disappointment, turned to her sobbing daughter and said gently, "Remember, dear, you are loved." It was the same sweet phrase that she had always used in parting from her daughters or kissing them good night.

Bird's own heart ached for the man that she loved, but she held her head high as she shepherded the two girls back to the Biltmore Hotel. A crowd of newsmen intercepted them to ask how she felt about the defeat. She replied with quiet dignity: "I wouldn't be saying what is true if I didn't say that I'm disappointed for my country. Lyndon would have made a noble President . . . a tough, can-do President. But as a mother and a wife and a woman who wakes up in the morning wanting to call her day her own, I have a sizeable feeling of relief."

The relief was short-lived. Lyndon met her back at the suite, and they sat up late rehashing the events of the memorable day with his leading backers. Both were bone tired by the time they finally went to bed, and they slept soundly.

"It was the best night's sleep I'd had in some time—what there was of it," Bird recalls with a smile. "Early the next morning the phone rang; it was for Lyndon. I had a mind to tell the caller that he was sleeping, but when the voice identified itself as Mr. Kennedy, I awakened Lyndon. That's when they first began to talk about his accepting the vice-presidency, and the first time that I had even considered such a possibility."

[75]

Johnson, after repeatedly telling his followers that he would not accept the Throttlebottom second place, was now confronted with the actual offer. Time was growing short, and the new party standard-bearer was prepared to put on pressure to get LBJ on the ticket.

"It was a very difficult decision," Bird muses softly. "Lyndon's personality and temperament are not exactly suited to being a number two man, and we thought that being a Senator from the state of Texas was just about as big a job as there was in the world. And, of course, his leadership was so outstanding! The Senate had been his spiritual and working home for twelve years. Think of leaving it for anything!"

Lyndon had only a few hours in which to decide. The Vice-president was to be chosen by the Convention that day, and the delegates were obviously going to elect whomever the new Presidential nominee wanted.

LBJ says of that crisis: "I had been through the heart attack, and I tried not to have my name go before the Convention, but Sam Rayburn and John Connally had it go, although we never felt like candidates. After Kennedy was nominated, the question was whether to go home and cry over spilt milk or to submerge myself in second place. Bird and I talked it out and agreed that a party which had done so much for us, and people who had worked so hard for us, deserved our help."

The decision was actually more complicated than the President makes it sound. He consulted with Speaker Rayburn and Connally, both of whom vehemently opposed his acceptance. Then the Kennedy pressure was applied directly on "Mr. Sam," who finally growled his consent for "my boy Lyndon" to join the ticket. He had come to realize that without LBJ on the slate, the Democrats might lose to the Republicans.

Bird agrees with Lyndon that he had not really expected to win the first-place nomination. Anybody who knows him, she says, "knows that if he had really yearned for it, he would have been working for it two years ahead of time, instead of announcing belatedly and half-heartedly, as if he had one hand tied behind his back."

In an analytical mood, she continues: "He couldn't work for it and be the majority leader at the same time, simply because there are only twenty-four hours in a day, and if you are a majority leader that is a full-time job. How do you plumb the depths of anybody else's heart, really? Even your own husband's? But to the best of my belief he wanted to do a good job as majority leader, rather than to run for the presidency.

"On the other hand, he is very responsive to the love, trust, and belief of those close to him. The two closest men in the world to him were Speaker Rayburn and John Connally, and both of them were determined to pull him into the presidency, if they had to haul him bucking and kicking. The vice-presidency just plain wasn't contemplated, at least by me. It was almost like asking me how I would like to go tomorrow to live in Egypt for the rest of my life."

Bird honestly does not know how much influence she personally had on Lyndon's decision to accept second place on the ticket. She says: "Both of us faced the reality that we had been working under the banner of the Democratic Party for twenty-four years and had been its frequent beneficiary. Now the time had come when Lyndon's decision could possibly be the deciding factor in whether the next administration would be Democratic or Republican. Could he shirk his duty?"

While the secret conferences between Lyndon, Mr. Sam, and the Kennedy team were in progress, Lynda and Lucy were blissfully unaware of the new crisis their parents faced. Having witnessed LBJ's defeat the evening before, and shed their tears of sympathy, they were now prepared to resume their status as Senatorial daughters. What better place to enjoy themselves, meanwhile, than Southern California?

With her mother's permission, Lynda Bird gaily set forth that morning with a beau to visit Disneyland. Lost in that delightful world of fantasy, she spent such a relaxing day that she arrived back in Los Angeles too late to hear her father's acceptance speech as vice-presidential nominee.

Recalling his displeasure at her absence on that historic occasion, which then seemed the pinnacle of his political career, Lynda laughs: "I was always Daddy's darling daughter, but I was not his darling daughter *that* evening."

But how could she have known that men, as well as women, are given to changing their minds?

Chapter

8

JACQUELINE KENNEDY did not attend the Convention at which her husband won the Presidential nomination. Her doctors had forbidden it, because the excitement of the 1956 Convention battle between John F. Kennedy and Estes Kefauver for the second place spot on the ticket had previously brought on a miscarriage.

Jackie and Lady Bird therefore had little more than a nodding acquaintance, when the Johnsons flew to Hyannis Port shortly after the Convention to help map campaign strategy. Both were Senatorial wives, but there was a seventeen-year difference in their ages. Their interests were consequently dissimilar, and the two women had met only occasionally at large parties.

Mrs. Kennedy was now pregnant again, and feeling none too sprightly when the Texans arrived at the big old beach house in the "Kennedy compound." Characteristically, Bird took the glamorous younger woman to her heart. While the party standard-bearers spoke in close huddles, Mrs. Johnson exclaimed appreciatively over Jackie's art work and the scrapbooks of photographs which the one-time "Inquiring Photographer" for a Washington newspaper had taken of family members and beach scenes.

After dinner, knowing that the men would want to talk business and that Jackie should rest, Bird diplomatically excused herself for the night. She started upstairs to the guest room, but almost immediately Mrs. Kennedy was at her side, saying miserably: "I feel dreadful. This is the most important time of Jack's life, and I'm doing nothing to help him. What can I do?"

The seasoned political trouper cast a practiced eye around the colorful, chintzy living room of the summer cottage and at the sketches by Jackie which were framed and hung on the walls.

Bird, too, had had a history of miscarriages, and it was with deep compassion that she replied: "Your house expresses you so very well. Why not ask newspaper people here individually to talk to you, and see it for themselves?"

A little later Lady Bird's eyes glowed as she praised the young woman whose husband had defeated Lyndon for the Presidential nomination. "I had met Jackie at large parties, but I didn't really know her well until we flew to Hyannis Port. I was simply charmed with what I saw. Her home shows love and attention. It has a cared-for air. She has talent and grace, and she is simply charming as a hostess. A scrapbook of photographs that she had taken showed remarkable artistry and craftsmanship. She would be a real asset in the White House."

The Democratic ticket, whose standard-bearers were less well known to the electorate than the Nixon-Lodge slate that was soon to be chosen by the Republican Convention, needed every vote that it could muster. Unfortunately, a rump session of Congress pinned Senators Kennedy and Johnson to their seats on Capitol Hill, when their time for campaigning was already short. Moreover, the session was proving so unproductive for measures which the Democrats had championed in their platform that it was becoming an embarrassment.

When the session eventually dragged to a close on August eighth, there was not a moment to lose. With Jackie permanently benched by her physicians for the duration of the campaign, Democratic strategists turned eagerly to Lady Bird as the party's answer to indefatigable Pat Nixon, a tried and proven Republican asset.

The Southern charmer was ready and willing to help. Throughout that frenetic fall, Bird smiled, drawled, and shook hands through thirty-five thousand miles of folksy whistle stops, feminine rallies, and TV appearances. Sun-up breakfasts and cold pancakes became daily fare for the quiet-voiced trouper, and "So glad all y'all came" became her campaign trade mark.

She spoke at hundreds of breakfasts, luncheons, tea parties, and press conferences, sometimes alone, but often with one or more of the "Kennedy ladies," as she called them, in tow. Mrs. Rose Kennedy, mother of the Presidential nominee, occasionally flew in alone. Eunice Kennedy Shriver, Jean Kennedy Smith, and Ethel Kennedy chatted their way through the clouds with Bird; and sprinted straight from the plane to the Johnson swimming pool whenever the "flying tea party" touched down at the LBJ ranch.

To launch the feminine political foray, Bird held a full-fledged press conference in Washington and wowed newsmen as well as women with her deft fielding of loaded questions. Asked if she thought Mr. Kennedy's Roman Catholic religion would affect Democratic chances, she sadly admitted that a religious issue did exist, but observed: "The more deeply one reads the Bible, and the more one thinks about it, the more fair he will be."

With a sparkle of humor she added that if the ticket ran into any real trouble on that score, Lyndon had "plenty of blood-kin Baptist relatives" who would come to the rescue. A newsman mentioned that Baylor University, the largest Baptist college in the world, seemed to present a hard core of opposition to a Catholic president, and Bird replied serenely: "Lyndon's great-grandfather was the second president of Baylor, and he converted Sam Houston. We still have the letter from Sam Houston to him. It's framed and hanging on the wall. If my house was on fire, I'd grab that letter on the way out."

A male questioner slyly asked her opinion of Jacqueline Kennedy's bouffant hair-do, which was undergoing critical scrutiny in the press, and Bird suavely retorted: "I think it's more important what's inside the head than what's outside." It was obvious she thought Jackie had plenty "inside."

When a newswoman sought to draw her out on the controversial issue of medical care for the aged, the Texas heiress was ready for that, too. Pointing out that her eighty-six-year-old father had been in and out of the hospital for a year, with two registered nurses in attendance, she said that he could afford to pay the "staggering" costs because he had "worked hard in a fruitful country," but that many of his neighbors and friends would have faced "financial ruin" through such an ordeal.

She then announced a breathless campaign schedule with the "Kennedy ladies" that would carry them to six Texas cities in the next three days. Just before leaving Washington, Bird sprained her ankle, but with it tightly bandaged, she merrily set forth in a chartered convair called "Lucy B," with a pilot nicknamed "Big Deal."

The first question that awaited her in Wichita Falls was whether her husband's role in the investigation of unions would hurt the ticket with labor. She replied smoothly that "many union members like my husband because of his battle against labor racketeers."

At a tremendous rally in Corpus Christi, Bird smilingly announced that Lyndon wanted the women "to do just five things" for him: "He wants you to write a card to all your kinfolks, have a coffee or tea party for your friends, phone ten people and ask each of them to phone ten more, write a letter to the editor of your newspaper, and drive a full car to the polls on November eighth."

The women were lapping up these unique rallies. The Southland had never seen anything to equal this glamorous petticoat brigade. The combination of Lady Bird's velvety drawl and the clipped Eastern accents of the chic Kennedy women was proving to be an irresistible lure, and women were turning out en masse. The Democrats had found a secret weapon.

In late September, Lyndon was getting dressed to attend a meeting of Baptist clergymen in Houston, at which Presidential candidate Kennedy would dramatically meet the challenge of his Catholic religion, when Bird was called to the telephone. Her friend Elizabeth Carpenter, who had been acting as her campaign press secretary, saw her flinch, pale perceptibly, and ask the voice at the other end of the wire: "Is that your decision? You are sure it's the right one? Very well, I'll be there in the morning."

Bird returned to the bedroom and said nothing to her husband as she helped him with his preparations. Ever a Stoic about her own suffering, she did not wish to disturb Lyndon just before such an important meeting. It was, in fact, Liz Carpenter who quietly told him that she and Bird would have to fly to Marshall.

"Oh, has the time come?" he asked sorrowfully, knowing that his greatly admired father-in-law was nearing the end in the Marshall hospital. Only two weeks before, without telling Bird, he had ordered his campaign plane stopped there briefly, so that he could pay a visit to the salty old gentleman who had helped him win his bride.

Bird and Liz stayed for two days at Marshall, while doctors sought to prolong Mr. Taylor's life by amputating a gangrenous leg. His daughter remained constantly at his bedside until the twelve-hour crisis had passed, and then went back to campaigning.

Each evening she telephoned the doctor, from whichever strange hotel was her brief stopping point, to check on her father's progress. By the time she reached Arizona, two weeks later, he was sinking rapidly, and she took time only to call Lyndon and their daughters before rushing back to the airport. Lynda and Lucy met her in Dallas, where she touched down briefly to give them a lift, and then continued the flight to Marshall.

"This may be the last time you will get to see your grandfather," she told them, and although they were saddened by the suffering of the old man with whom they had spent many happy vacations, they were so overjoyed at the unexpected reunion with their mother that they poured out their news of dates, parties, and school activities in a jumble of words.

"Lady Bird sat there and glowed," Liz says. "I realized then how deeply she had been missing the joy of her children's chatter, while maintaining her rigid campaign schedule. This was the best occupational therapy that she could have had at such a time."

Once again the indomitable Tom Taylor rallied, and once more his valiant daughter returned to the campaign trail. The cities rushed by in a kaleidoscope of colorful oratory, banners, and tea parties. Bird smilingly shook a never-ending line of outstretched hands, but her heart was often with her father, even though she always placed Lyndon's interests first.

After a whistle-stopping trip across Tennessee, Bird made her headquarters in Washington for a few days while filling speaking engagements in nearby Virginia and Delaware. She was also arranging with the "Kennedy ladies" for a second swing through Texas, and calling the Marshall hospital each evening to talk with her father's nurse and doctor.

"Mr. Boss" had taken a critical turn and the end was imminent, but Bird stoically told no one except a few intimate friends. She did not want the women who had worked so valiantly on behalf of the Kennedy-Johnson ticket to worry, just because she was so worried. Her only surviving brother, Antonio Taylor, was already en route from his home in Sante Fe to Marshall, and as soon as her engagements were completed, Bird and her long-time Texas friend, Mary Rather, flew to Marshall, leaving Liz Carpenter behind to complete arrangements for the Texas tour with J.F.K.'s sisters and sisters-in-law.

For two days, Bird scarcely left her father's bedside. During this sad period, Mary Rather took a pair of Lady Bird's campaigning shoes to have the heel caps replaced, and the shoemaker confided that he had been "repairing Lady Bird's shoes since she was a little girl." The hospital gave Bird and Mary a small room with a telephone, so that they could keep in touch with Liz and with Lyndon's staff.

In mid-afternoon of October twenty-second, Mary was poring over schedules when Bird came to the door. Tears overflowed as she said quietly: "My daddy has just died. Will you please try to locate Lyndon?"

She immediately regained her composure, and by the time her husband was on the other end of the wire, she was pleading with him not to come "until just in time for the funeral." To Mary she explained that "Lyndon suffers so at funerals."

Her urging was to no avail. "No, I want to be there with you," Lyndon said; and he came immediately, even as his two daughters were flying down from Washington to be met in Shreveport by Mary Rather.

The neighbors, as usual at such times in small towns, rose beautifully to the occasion. Women of the Karnack Methodist Church brought homemade pies, cakes, covered dishes, and baked hams, and the "Brick House" was soon overflowing with food for the out-of-town mourners.

Bird talked quietly with old friends of her strong, erect, courtly father, of the picnics at Caddo Lake, the fishing

trips and boat rides among the timeless cypress trees growing out of the water, and of the ugly crocodiles in the lake.

Funeral services were held at the Methodist church,
which stood on land donated by "Mr. Boss" and which had
a Taylor fellowship wing endowed by him. Across the
highway stood the Baptist church, and to the east the
Church of Christ. Mr. Taylor, although a Methodist, had
given them both their land, just as he had also provided
free land on which the elementary and high schools stood.

Because "Mr. Boss" had married again shortly after
Bird's own wedding, he was not buried beside her mother
in the tenderly cared for little Confederate cemetery at
Scottsville; but it was big Tom Taylor who had inscribed
on Minnie Pattillo Taylor's headstone: "Forgetful of self,
she lived only for others."

Bird's friends commented on how well that inscription
fitted Minnie's daughter, too. She remained with her
brother, Tony, for only one more day after her husband
and daughters departed in order to attend to family matters. Then, because she knew that Lyndon's cause required
her help, she and Mary Rather flew to San Antonio at night
to rejoin the ladies tea party brigade. There was now no
time for tears.

Chapter

9

THE CAMPAIGN was heading into the home stretch, and Bird's powder-puff contingency pressed on into less familiar territory. In Fort Wayne, Indiana, her plane was supposed to rendezvous briefly with that of Vice-presidential candidate Johnson, but his arrival was delayed, and she flew on without seeing him.

"I got to see a nice crowd at the airport all by myself," she said smilingly, to mask her disappointment at missing her husband. She had just arrived at Charlotte, North Carolina, for the next engagement. "But I was awfully sorry that Lyndon inconvenienced those nice people who were waiting."

Mrs. Joseph P. Kennedy flew into Charlotte by commercial plane from Hot Springs, Arkansas, and the two women joined forces at an enthusiastic coffeeklatch. When surprised reporters commented on her fresh appearance, in view of her frenzied schedule, Bird gallantly replied that "campaigning might be tiring, if it weren't so much fun." She added that her own sympathies lay with her husband and Mr. Kennedy, "because they have to do the heavy thinkin'."

A near tragedy in Greensboro, North Carolina, left her traveling companions with frazzled nerves, but not the indomitable Lady Bird. Landing in heavy fog, with almost zero visibility, her campaign plane skidded beyond the airstrip into a neighboring field. Fortunately, it did not overturn and burn. Unperturbed, the woman who once hated flying stepped out and began blithely shaking each of two thousand hands.

With admirable understatement, she calmly told a waiting press conference that she was "mighty glad to be in North Carolina, and glad to be on firm ground again." Then she calmly re-entered the plane and flew on to Fayetteville, where she made a speech that evening.

Back in Washington for a brief stopover, to repack her well-worn wardrobe, and give her teenage daughters "a little mothering," she received me for an exclusive interview. Over a cup of coffee on the screened verandah overlooking her small garden, I drew her out about her feminine rivals on the Republican ticket. Typically, the soft-spoken Southern woman could find nothing but good to say about them. Of her opposite number, Mrs. Henry Cabot Lodge, she bubbled: "I've had a simply delightful experience with the Lodges, even though I don't know them as well as I'd like to. When Lyndon addressed the

United Nations in New York two years ago the Lodges were our hosts, and they couldn't have been more informal, friendly, and delightful. They're just top-notch!"

Of Patricia Nixon, who was vigorously campaigning with her Presidential-aspirant husband on the opposition ticket, Bird said: "I think Pat does a very fine job. As a Senate wife, I appreciate her conscientious and devoted attention to being our presiding officer every Tuesday at the Senate Ladies' Red Cross unit."

She talked in equally disarming terms about her husband's probable role if the Kennedy-Johnson team should win in November. "I have a feeling that each man can set his own pattern to a sizeable extent as Vice-president," she drawled. "Something tells me that if Lyndon is elected, he'll make his new job one of the busiest in the capital." Her words were later, of course, to prove prophetic.

Bird professed to have lost all fears for her husband's health. "Having lived through what he has these last few months," she remarked pensively, "I have no worries about his heart any more."

I asked about her own possible role as Second Lady, and she sipped coffee thoughtfully before replying: "Whoever becomes Second Lady will continue to be the same person she was before. If she liked to run a house and help her husband and children, she will keep right on doing the same, except that her husband's job will have expanded. He will set the pattern and she will fit into it." Bird, of course had always fitted into Lyndon's pattern.

Lynda Bird, sixteen, and Lucy Baines, thirteen, occasionally wandered in and out to consult their mother about clothes, dates, and schedules. She responded to their interruptions with saintly calm. I asked what effect she felt the spotlight of the Vice-presidency might have on the girls, and she thoughtfully said: "I believe they're safe. This is a subject to which I've given a lot of thought, but it *is* a problem, because they want more of our attention and companionship than we've been able to give them in recent years. Lyndon and I are both saddened by that fact." Bird smilingly admitted that "we have the usual teenage problems, with the girls on the telephone all the time and never remembering to pick up their clothes, but, generally speaking, they're highly satisfactory girls."

Mention of the telephone was particularly apt. Just as our interview began, Lucy Baines had burst dramatically onto the verandah, wailing, "Mother, you've ruined my whole life! You had the telephone tied up all morning, when *he* might have been trying to invite me to lunch."

To a thirteen-year-old Junior Miss the tragedy was real, and Bird patiently apologized for having made those essential calls. She explained to me that Lucy had met a new page boy at the Capitol a few days before, and was naturally hoping that he would pursue her. Unfortunately, no call came for Lucy during the hour I was there, even though the line was now free. Finally, Lucy decided to take matters into her own hands. She sounded a great deal like her activist father as she announced that she would go down to his office, in the hope that she might run into the page boy.

Lady Bird gave her permission, and I offered her a lift part way in my car. As we drove away from the house, Lucy exclaimed excitedly, "Somehow I just can't get over boys beginning to pay attention to me. You see, I was always a wallflower."

Smiling nostalgically at the growing-up pangs of a thirteen-year-old girl, I tried to reassure her, but she sighed: "At the parties, none of the boys ask me to dance, even though I'm a very good dancer. I used to win prizes. I was flabbergasted when a boy actually asked me to go out for a Coke with him. I couldn't believe it was true!"

She carefully adjusted the pleats on her brand-new dress and asked anxiously if I thought she would look all right for the possible meeting. "I have another new dress that shows me off a little better," she confided, "but he saw me in that yesterday. Yesterday was one of those terrible days when everything went wrong. He had actually asked me to meet him at the Capitol for lunch—our first real date—and to make sure I'd be on time I went shopping two whole hours early.

"Then . . ." The stark horror of it slowed her speech for a moment. "Then I caught my heel in the elevator at the store and broke it off completely. It made me twenty whole minutes late, and I know he thought I had stood him up."

Her voice sank almost to a whisper. "He took it all right, but I'm sure he must be mad, because he said he'd call me last night and he didn't. I spent the evening making cookies, and . . ."

Jerking around in the car to look me in the eye, she exclaimed, "Mrs. Montgomery, I know I did wrong, but having been a wallflower for so long, it's terribly hard for me to play hard-to-get. I finally called *him* and told him I'd made some brownies, and he said fine, maybe he'd stop around later today and help me eat them. I tried to be casual, too, but what if he's been trying to phone me while Mother was taking all those long-distance calls?"

She subsided into abject misery, but soon bubbled, "I was real proud of the way I acted when he called to invite me for lunch yesterday. He asked was I coming to the Capitol, and I said no. He said yes you are; you're going to have lunch with me.

"I said I didn't know whether I was free; I'd have to look at my date book. Of course, I knew I didn't have a thing in it, but I walked away from the phone and came back to say it was OK."

She smiled in happy remembrance at her arch sophistication. Then her face clouded and she muttered, "If only I hadn't broken off that heel and been late yesterday! That's why I'm wearing these old flat-heeled shoes today."

We rode along in silence for a moment, until she suddenly exclaimed, "Darn heredity, anyway!"

Her tone was so explosive that I asked what in the world that remark signified.

"It's my feet," she said wrathfully. "Mother has exactly the same kind. Our heels are about triple-triple-triple-A, and how can you ever make shoes stay on when they don't come that narrow in the heels?"

Her trim little figure, already beginning to show her womanly curves, looked adorable to me. To her, it was a mess. With infinite dissatisfaction, she murmured, "My bust is thirty-two, and my waist is twenty-seven, but I'm not even going to tell you what my hips measure. They just keep going out."

As we neared the corner where she could change to a cab, I asked if she thought life would be more fun if her father became Vice-president.

Sighing heavily, she said, "Oh, I imagine it would be about the same."

To cheer her up, I suggested that she would probably be moving to a larger house in that event.

She gave me the kind of a look that is usually reserved for an idiot child. Disgust dripped from her healthy pink tongue as she exploded, "Wellllll, we *won't!* Mother and Daddy have been talking about it for years, but they never do a single thing about it!"

Thirteen is always a difficult growing-up age, seemingly fraught with tragedies. Lucy was actually a normal, lovable young girl beset by the usual frustrations of the early teens. She was talented and dramatically inclined. She doted on poetry, and wrote long poems of her own. She loved her piano lessons, and composed music. At Camp Mystic, where she spent each summer, she excelled in arts, crafts, and interpretive dancing. She edited the Camp newspaper, and frequently served as chaplain of her tribe because she could "pray so well" when called upon unexpectedly.

How happy she would have been, in that Fall of 1960, if she could have known that within a year she would move to a gracious Washington mansion, and within three years to the White House. What a pity that she could not then have foreseen the poised, slim-hipped, sixteen-year-old Lucy of 1964, who would charm foreign visitors with her gracious hospitality, and be able to pick-and-choose among the handsome college boys who eagerly sought her company. But this was still in the future.

Lady Bird counseled lovingly with the two girls before hitting the campaign trail again. In Lexington, Kentucky, she and Mrs. Rose Kennedy stood for two hours shaking hands, and then answered questions at a packed rally that evening. While Bird was speaking, a member of the audience emitted a crowing-rooster sound, and she wrinkled her forehead in puzzlement. Not realizing that "crowing" was an old Democratic custom in Fayette County, she drawled: "That sounds like one of those beagle dogs we have down home."

Having touched down earlier that same day in Raleigh, North Carolina, and Louisville, Kentucky, she remarked: "If I didn't enjoy this, I'd be in the wrong business, wouldn't I?" Commenting on the address that Rose Kennedy had just delivered, she exclaimed: "The moment I heard her speech, I knew I was travelin' in tall cotton!"

Seldom in American history had there been a more folksy campaign for the nation's two highest offices, and certainly never such a one on the distaff side. Bird was as unaffected as a field of Texas bluebonnets, and the unexpected warmth of her approach was making an obvious hit with Southern and Midwestern women.

Now she flew on to sophisticated New York City, where she told a big-league press conference that "campaignin' has priority at this time, and food and sleep just have to wait." Asked for her appraisal of the Kennedy-Johnson chances, she replied candidly: "I can judge only what I see, and my hands and feet tell me that the prospects are awfully good."

A reporter asked how she had managed to stay out of the then-raging controversy between Jackie Kennedy and Pat Nixon over which spent the most on her clothes. With a shy smile she replied: "I guess I'm pretty unremarkable as far as clothing goes. No Paris, alas."

Lyndon was scheduled to appear on the *Today* television show at 8:00 A.M., but when he awakened with a sore throat and husky voice, Bird telephoned Attorney Leonard Marks, who was handling LBJ's radio-TV schedule. "I don't imagine Dave Garroway would want me as a substitute," she began hesitantly, "but I hate to disappoint him about Lyndon, so if you want to take me along as a volunteer I would be willing to do anything you think I could."

Marks picked her up at the Biltmore Hotel and escorted her to the studio. "Please don't feel embarrassed about not having me, if you can fill in with someone else," she said humbly, as she greeted Garroway.

She went on for fifteen minutes, without preparation, and stole the show.

Georgia Democrats declared a "Lady Bird Johnson Day," and with her never-flagging smile she flew in for a political dinner at the farm of Senator Herman Talmadge, located near Lovejoy. It was joy, indeed, for Dixie-bred Bird. The menu not only included Talmadge country ham but the hominy grits that she had been missing.

Perhaps the high spot of Lady Bird's campaign came in mid-October, when she joined Lyndon for an LBJ Victory Special train trip through her mother's home state of Alabama. This was "kissin' kin" territory, and as the train pulled into Montgomery, she dashed onto the rear platform to greet her blood kin who had come to welcome her. At almost every whistle stop thereafter, Bird found long-lost "cousins" in the milling crowds. In fact, the twelve-car special train soon began to groan beneath the weight of relatives and politicians who climbed aboard.

The LBJ Victory Special also had Lucy Baines in tow for the two days in kinfolk territory. Then it chugged on across the Southland in a 3,500-mile trek that drew to a climax in a New Orleans extravaganza. Airplanes were re-boarded, and the states ticked off in rapid succession. Bird attended "bean feeds" on the banks of the Wabash and plowing contests in Iowa.

Flying into Delaware, she told a Wilmington audience

that her formula for relaxing was to "put my mind on a restful scene." The one she usually chose was the mental image of her view from the front porch of the LBJ ranch, with white-faced Herefords grazing in the rolling pastures.

Governor Abe Ribicoff introduced her in Hartford, Connecticut, as "the right kind of wife for a man whose name will go down in history." By that time she had personally met a hundred thousand women in thirty states, and was still selling Lyndon. "He's the kind of a man who can get things done," she would say. "He strives for the best, and he does the possible."

At a televised press conference in the Governor's mansion at Hartford, she modestly sidestepped a question about Quemoy-Matsu by saying: "I simply know I'm not as smart as I ought to be on foreign policy."

Her innate simplicity and sincerity charmed the women as no boastful political speech could have done. A reporter asked how she managed her wardrobe problem with such a heavy travel schedule, and she said frankly: "When I get back to Washington, I'll take these clothes I've been wearing to the dry cleaners. Since he doesn't work Saturdays, I'll have to wait until next week to get them, but I can pick up some that I left for cleaning the last time I was home. Then I'll be ready to join Lyndon in Missouri."

When a newswoman asked her dress size, she confided that during the months following Lyndon's heart attack she had lost twenty pounds, and the size dropped from a fourteen to a ten. She liked herself so much better that way, she added, that she had been dieting since.

The campaign was nearing its climax, and as her plane touched down in Chicago, Bird announced that she scented victory in the air. Asked whether she was tired after two solid months of campaigning, she laughed and shrugged. "Frankly, yes. But it hardly behooves me to be tired, when I know a whole lot of people are putting a lot more into it than I am." Her colloquialisms fascinated Chicago newsmen. Most of them had never before heard her favorite similes: "As busy as a man killin' snakes"—"As noisy as a mule in a tin barn"—"The kind of people who'd charge hell with a bucket of water."

Only two personal heartaches marred that historic campaign for Lady Bird. The first was her father's death. The other was a shocking mob scene that occurred in Dallas.

In the last week of the campaign, a group of "ugly Americans," carried away by partisan emotionalism, tried to bar the path of the Vice-presidential nominee and his wife as they sought to enter the Adolphus Hotel for a rally. The streets were jammed to capacity with placard-waving opponents, and words like "traitor" and "yankee" caught their eye. Some of the signs accused Lyndon of selling out the South, and a few were aimed at Bird herself.

"It was a mighty noisy, articulate, and hate-filled segment of the Dallas community," she says. "My main feeling was one of absolute incredulity. I couldn't believe this was Texas. I couldn't believe this was home, where I had gone to school as a girl. But it was only a small segment of Dallas."

She remembers seeing Republican Representative Bruce Alger of Dallas in the throng. "He's quite a tall man, very easily visible, and he was in the front ranks," she says and winces. "I guess it's the same feeling one has about war. You don't believe it's really happening. But, personally, I felt quite steely. I knew I had to keep walking and suppress all emotions. I felt no fear whatsoever. Rather, it was utter incredulity and a sort of anger that I knew must be kept pent-up inside. I felt some hurt, too, remembering that these were people for whom we'd been working for twelve years."

As usual, Bird interrupted her narrative to praise her husband. "I must say," she added, "that Lyndon was nine times steelier than I was. I think he felt that once he was in this spitting, screaming crowd he would make the most of it. I just never saw him look more erect or more dignified or more determined. By contrast he made them look mighty small."

A few in the well-dressed mob spat at them, and someone deliberately mussed Bird's hair. She gave no outward sign of awareness, and when she and Lyndon finally reached the door to the ballroom, where the rally was being held, she calmly took out her comb and ran it through her tousled hair. Her grim smile matched her husband's.

Newspapers reported the shocking scene widely, and most Texans were outraged. There is little doubt but that the unsportsmanlike behavior of the mob and the calm dignity of the Johnsons helped to put the doubtful Lone Star State into the Democratic column.

On election eve, Bird and Lyndon checked in at the Driskill Hotel in Austin. It was the scene of their first date, but now they had other things on their minds. Ignoring her own weariness, Bird made the rounds with Lyndon to his several campaign headquarters to thank party workers for their service.

The next day, after voting in Johnson City, they returned to Austin to await the returns. Bird curled up on a divan and took out a pencil and paper. Occasionally she scratched out words as she wrote, but at last she completed two statements. By morning she would be needing one or the other, depending on the verdict of the voters.

The "losing" statement, which did not need to be used, said simply: "This has been a most dramatic episode in my life, one I will always cherish, to have known the whole United States, just as I have cherished all these twenty-four years of knowing Texas. Now, we'll go back to applying ourselves to the job at hand. To all the people who have marched beside us in our twenty-four years of public life, and to the thousands of women I met along the campaign trail who have worked so hard, we are deeply grateful."

Lady Bird and Lyndon sat up late into the night, surrounded by intimate friends from many previous campaigns. It was a close race, the closest presidential contest in the history of America, but by four A.M. the Democrats apparently had won.

Television picked up the image of Pat Nixon weeping, and Bird's heart reached out to her. Knowing how deeply a devoted wife shares her husband's disappointments, Bird said aloud: "I wish I could say something to help her feel better."

Lyndon Baines Johnson had not only won election as Vice-president, but re-election to the Senate as well. His defeated Senate opponent was Republican John Tower of Wichita Falls, a University teacher who was soon in a special election, to capture the Senate seat from which Lyndon would have to resign. For the first time since Reconstruction days, a GOP Senator would win at the polls in the South.

The morning after the November eighth Presidential election, newsmen visited the Johnsons in their hotel suite. The Vice-president-elect was in slacks and a red polo shirt.

When reporters asked Bird about their plans, she replied jauntily: "We are going back to the ranch tomorrow and be just plain vegetables for a few days."

She meant it when she said it, but it was impossible for her mother-heart to vegetate. Lynda and Lucy were in Washington, eager to hear all, so instead of going to the ranch she flew North. From the airport she went straight home to bed, and was having dinner there an hour later when a reporter telephoned.

"I got to missin' the girls," Bird drawled in explanation of her changed plans. "I never laid eyes on the ranch, the weather was so bad. It rained and rained."

That was all she had to say about the heroic part she had played in the hard-fought victory that fall. It was Campaign Manager Robert Kennedy who dotted the "i."

Said the brother of the President-elect: "Lady Bird carried Texas for us."

Chapter

10

DURING the hiatus between election and Inauguration Day, the Johnsons finally found a little time to relax at the ranch. Politicians and newsmen, however, were soon beating a path to the idyllic hideaway.

"This is our heart's home," Bird would tell visitors as she escorted them through the rambling, twelve-room ranchhouse. She took special pride in pointing out the office, which is called the "Friendship Memento Room." Its most prominent feature is a huge mahogany desk that Lyndon used at the Senate when he was minority leader. It was later purchased for him as a gift from his staff.

A silver saddle presented to him by President Lopez Mateos of Mexico is suspended from the front of the stone fireplace, and Bird points it out, along with the pedigrees of two Tennessee walking horses.

The room is a clutter of gifts and keepsakes. On the wall hangs a plaque of semi-precious stones in the shape of the North and South American continents, with a portrait of Lyndon in silver. A group of Mexican organizations presented it to him during a pre-campaign trip to Acapulco. Gavels and centennial plates adorn the bookshelves behind Lyndon's big desk.

The green-and-orange living room is the oldest part of the original ranchhouse, which was built by Lyndon's great-grandfather. Behind its thick walls his ancestors ate, slept, and lived a pioneer life. The master bedroom, in soft green and white, features an oil portrait of Bird, and a door leads outside to Lyndon's heated swimming pool, the one added after his heart attack.

In an upstairs bedroom is a marble-topped dresser belonging to Lyndon's mother, and childhood pictures of the family, including a portrait of Lady Bird at age fifteen. She had bobbed black hair and a soulful expression. Down the hall is "the best bedroom," where such dignitaries as President and Mrs. Lopez Mateos, Adlai Stevenson, and practically a quorum of the Senate have slept.

All of the furnishings are homey and lived with. In the six bedrooms are individual television sets, placed at the foot of each bed for viewing in solid comfort. Every room has piped-in music, complete with a loudspeaker system, which is also carried to the swimming pool and nearby corral, so that LBJ can issue orders to anyone who is not stone deaf when the whim seizes him.

The Johnson's own bedroom is simply furnished with a mahogany double bed, a double dresser, and a rocking chair. Its ample walk-in closet is neatly divided between Lyndon and Bird, and holds a collection of Lyndon's broad-

brimmed Stetson hats. The extroverted politician sometimes sailed these hats into a rally, but since they cost
twenty-five dollars apiece, he paid a boy a dollar to retrieve
them. The effect was just as dramatic, but he saved money.

The main ranch, encompassing over four hundred acres,
is located thirteen miles west of Johnson City, a one-time
frontier outpost that was named for Lyndon's forebears.
It was a center of Indian fighting and two thick stone forts
still stand near the ranch. Thin slits in their walls provided
for defensive rifle fire against the warring tribes.

The original ranchhouse was built at the same time as
the forts and is now the Johnson living room. A short dis-
tance down the road is the three-room frame cottage where
Lyndon was born. His mother, a city-bred girl who hated
the isolation of the ranch, used to flinch when her son
pointed out to visitors the little hut where she was taken
as a bride. The family doesn't own it now, and itinerate
Mexican families have occupied it from time to time, but
the irrepressible Lyndon invariably shows visiting heads
of states and other distinguished visitors "where I got my
start."

Nearby is a stone-walled cemetery where Lyndon's parents and other ancestors are buried. It lies close by the
Pedernales River, shaded by ancient live oak trees and
purple sage.

In the years since the original purchase, Bird has gradually acquired eighteen hundred adjoining acres of haunt-
ingly beautiful wild land, where white-tailed deer bound
gracefully through the timber. Lyndon's very soul seems
to meld with this lovely terrain. As he surveys his grazing
lands, the white-faced Herefords, the dammed river, and
the timberland, he observes with deep satisfaction: "A

man could make a living here. If I ever had to, this working ranch is where I'd live."

A few years after acquiring the ranch, Lyndon decided to take up deer hunting. Bird was so delighted that her hard-working husband was at last showing an interest in a hobby that she, too, learned to shoot a rifle, with which she usually bags her quota each fall.

Lyndon's idea of a hunting trip, however, is a mechanized safari in a fleet of air-conditioned cars equipped with intercommunications systems. He drives his cars as if they were cow ponies, and once, as Bird was following with guests at the wheel of the second car, trying to match his ninety-mile-an-hour pace, he suddenly zoomed up a forty-five-degree embankment. As he did so, he bellowed gleefully into the intercom: "Bird, you don't have to come up here if you're scared to try."

With her usual serenity she replied: "Of course, I'm coming, darling." Her companions gritted their teeth while her car shot smoothly up the earth dam that was barely wide enough for the wheelbase.

The future President was always something of a daredevil, and as Eleanor Roosevelt did, he enjoys driving fast. He loves gadgets and every type of airplane. During a flood of the Pedernales River one year, which uprooted his prize pecan trees, he and a pilot, Ray Goodwin, went out in a helicopter to evacuate stranded neighbors. Despite the dangerously rising waters, one old woman refused to leave without her dog, so Lyndon over her protests insisted on ushering her to the 'copter. Then he went back for her dog. It bit him.

The servants on the ranch are long time employees, who have learned to expect the unexpected from Lyndon. During his Vice-presidential campaign, he once conned Bird into telephoning the long-suffering help to "prepare every bed on the place" for the eighteen newsmen who were accompanying him in his private plane. What they all needed, he decided, was a good night's sleep at the ranch.

Lady Bird, who was reared with the East Texas plantation background of magnolias and cotton, does not pretend to have quite the same spiritual affinity for the Western-style ranch as Lyndon, but she has grown to understand its operations. Touching down there briefly during the 1960 campaign, she was gazing out at the flood-swollen Pedernales River, when a sad-faced Hereford lowed near the cattle guard.

"Why, he's favoring his right foot," she exclaimed compassionately. "I must tell the foreman about it right away."

Had Bird not chosen, early in her married life, to accommodate herself to Lyndon's every wish, she would probably be a decidedly different person today. She likes stage plays and movies, and has a wide interest in literature. Lyndon regards all such things as a waste of time. Her idea of a relaxing evening is a game of bridge, but she indulges herself in that pastime no oftener than two or three times a year.

A woman with less character could have become a mere shadow of such an overwhelming man as Lyndon Baines Johnson, but Bird has managed to retain her own perspective and personality. As Mary Rather, LBJ's one-time Congressional secretary has said: "The most remarkable thing about Bird is that although she has subordinated herself to Lyndon's wishes and way of life, she has remained a well-rounded individual. He is so dominating and forceful that he could easily have overshadowed her, but she has not permitted that to happen. She is a complete and total person."

The President admits that he has "never seen Bird mad but twice in my life." The first time was in 1942, when he had ignored her excited announcement that she had found her dream house. The other occurred when they were riding along a trail in the hilly terrain of the ranch. Impatient as ever, Lyndon gave her horse a sharp prod and the startled animal leaped so suddenly that Bird nearly lost her balance.

"I'll manage my own horse, thank you," was all that she said, but LBJ has never forgotten the look that accompanied the remark.

Behind the composed façade of Lady Bird Johnson lies a woman of spirit, who is sometimes weary of the "smiling image" that she presents to the world. Her humor is low key, but it is there, bubbling just beneath the surface.

In fact, after Lyndon's election to the Vice-presidency, she became so bored with reading the bland, innocuous articles about herself that she remarked to a friend with a pixie grin, "They make me feel like putting on red tights and running down Pennsylvania Avenue."

It was a neat twist on a comment which Jacqueline Kennedy had made about her shortly before. Having observed Bird's apparent indulgence of Lyndon's every whim, Jackie declared, "If Lyndon asked her to, Bird would walk naked down Pennsylvania Avenue."

The time was steadily approaching when the four of them—President and Mrs. Kennedy, Vice-president and Mrs. Johnson—would ride in style down that historic avenue in a snow-blitzed Inaugural parade.

Chapter

11

LADY BIRD'S devoted claque of admirers sometimes smiles indulgently over her penchant for saving a dime. Even as the wife of the Senate majority leader—a position which Lyndon had made into the second most powerful in the nation—his wife would purchase balcony tickets for herself at the theater when he had business engagements. She rode coach trains to New York and tourist planes to Texas.

She bought seconds in towels and linens, shopped for dresses at out-of-season sales, and required three competitive bids before making any modernizations in the house.

No one has ever been able to accuse her, however, of stinginess with her family and friends. The Inauguration of 1961 was a case in point. Now that the hard-fought victory had been won, Bird was determined that old friends who had shared their campaign heartaches should also sample the joy. Since ball gowns are seldom needed in small Texas and Alabama towns, and some of the relatives and friends were unable to afford such extravagances, Bird quietly paid for the dresses.

The day of the Inauguration dawned white and bitingly cold. On Inauguration eve, one of the heaviest snowfalls in Washington's recorded history had turned the streets into virtually impassable chasms, and had so effectively stalled traffic that official parties planned for hundreds boasted only twelve to twenty shivering guests. Lyndon and Lady Bird Johnson, however, smiled their way that evening through the long Inaugural gala, staged by Frank Sinatra and other Hollywood friends of Peter Lawford, the President-elect's actor brother-in-law.

The next noon, unmindful of the bitter chill, Bird stood glowingly beside her tall husband on the steps of the United States Capitol, while he and President Kennedy swore to uphold the Constitution, their breath frosting on their lips. Amazing Lyndon! Long ago, in Gene Boehringer's office at the Texas Capitol, when he first strolled into her life, Bird "knew I had met something remarkable, but I didn't know quite what." Now she knew!

Three years later, talking with her at the White House, I asked the First Lady to recall her reflections on that momentous day in their lives. In her modest way, she began: "It was chiefly of the great pageantry of this country; of all the branches of government assembled, and all the types of brains and talents and achievement that were gathered there on that platform, and in the sea of faces; and wondering how we were going to fit in; and knowing it was going to be different from the twenty-four years in Congress from which we were cutting ourselves off.

"I felt a yearning to help Robert Frost get through with that poem, and then there was almost a feeling of laughter about the man who was crouched in the aisle with the fire apparatus, as steam was rising from the podium. He was just about to let it blow at the flames, but people were whispering, 'No, no, not yet.' It did not seem like quite the time to do it, while a prayer was going on. I felt a whole galaxy of emotions."

That evening, with television cameras spotlighting the new heads of our country wherever they went, the nation not only discovered the glamorous beauty of thirty-one-year-old Jacqueline Kennedy but the smooth éclat of forty-seven-year-old Lady Bird Johnson as well.

The petite, graceful Southern woman wore a sleeveless gown of coral brocade and clutched a white fox shoulder scarf that her husband had given her for their twenty-fifth wedding anniversary the year before. Television viewers could not fail to notice how she lovingly turned to give the spotlight to Lyndon and their two vivacious daughters, and how she gamely continued at her husband's side until the last of the five balls had been visited, although the convalescing First Lady had had to miss the final two.

A new world now gaped open to admit the Johnsons of Texas. From the moment of Lyndon's Inauguration, Secret Service agents were constantly on guard. Irrepressible Lucy Baines made their acquaintance on the round of Inaugural balls and chirped: "I've never been so thoroughly chaperoned in my whole life."

Within a matter of days sixteen-year-old Lynda Bird, who was attending the National Cathedral School for Girls, started to receive dance invitations from boys she had never met. She began to feel uncomfortable when they introduced her as "the Vice-president's daughter" instead of as Lynda Johnson. Although she had inherited her father's dramatic flair, she had enough of her mother's practicality to wonder whether they liked her for herself or for her father's new position.

Bird had now recovered from the virus which, briefly, confined the intrepid trouper to bed a few days before the Inaugural festivities. She and her daughters had purchased their Inaugural ball gowns at Nieman-Marcus in Dallas during the Christmas holidays, and in the intervening three weeks, before she became Second Lady, she described her activities in this quaint, old-fashioned way: "I'm trying to draw together all the threads of my life, and make sure that all my kinfolks and Alabama cousins are invited to the Inauguration. I keep having dreams that I might forget my shoes, or some of my oldest and dearest friends."

Lucy Baines was entertaining another kind of dream. A week before he was to "lay down my vote for a gavel," the Senate majority leader was busily pouring over the papers on his big desk when his telephone rang. The rangy Texan ignored it as long as possible, and then grabbed for its clamorous throat. Obviously the call must be important or it could never have been cleared through his efficient staff.

"Daddy," sighed a soft, familiar voice, "you'll just have to come and help me. I've found the most heavenly suit, but it might be just a little too sophisticated for me."

The Vice-president-elect grinned and began to unwind. His desk pad was crowded with appointments, but here was a challenge that obviously called for the expert kind of advice that only he was qualified to give. Buzzing for his secretary, he explained the crisis and headed for a Washington department store. Lucy and Lynda were both await-ing him in the ready-to-wear department.

This was the first time that they had ever summoned their father, without mother along, to pass judgment on feminine purchases. They knew by experience, however, that whenever Lady Bird met Lyndon at a shop, he invari-ably bought more than she had intended.

The big man from Johnson City took immediate com-mand of the situation. After giving it some judicious thought, he decided that the four-piece blue wool suit with matching sport coat was exactly right for Lucy. Talking about his purchases with fatherly pride at a party that eve-ning he declared: "Why, it wasn't too sophisticated at all! Lucy is the only one in our family with blue eyes, so the suit looked like it was just made for her."

Bird, of course, was more adept at seeing through her daughter's wiles. When chatting about it afterward, she smiled and said ruefully: "I just can't get over Lucy worry-ing about anything in the world being too sophisticated for her. She's been bulldozing me for too long, and trying to get into clothes more grown up than she is."

The ruse, however, worked exactly as Lucy had fore-seen. Not only did Lyndon buy Lynda Bird a similar suit in beige, but he also purchased new negligees for both girls. With this step, Bird was in hearty agreement.

"He filled a need that I should have performed for them a long time ago," she said indulgently. "The poor little souls didn't have anything decent to cover their backs in the way of a bathrobe, so Lyndon bought them spectacular gold-colored ones that match."

Bird approached her new duties as Second Lady with the same intensity that she had shown when, as a bride, she was learning to cook. To an interviewer who asked how she conceived of her new role, she replied with her usual self-effacement: "Helping Lyndon all that I can, helping Mrs. Kennedy whenever she needs me, and becoming a more alive me."

To implement the last-named goal, she almost immediately launched a Spanish conversation class at her house. It was time, she decided, that she learned to speak another language well. She and five other officials' wives now hired Professor Elsa Lopez McGuire to conduct their group.

A blackboard became a permanent fixture in the family quarters, and for the next three years Bird allowed nothing but good-will trips or other official duties to interrupt the schedule of three-day-a-week classes from nine until eleven-thirty A.M. Soon she became so proficient that she could deliver charming little speeches in Spanish, when greeting visitors from south of the Rio Grande.

It was only a matter of days after the Inauguration before Bird became the number one pinch-hitter for First Lady Jacqueline Kennedy, who was still recuperating from the birth of a son the previous Thanksgiving. She also devoted nearly every Tuesday to the Senate Ladies' Red Cross unit, over which she now presided, as the wife of the Vice-president, in her crisp white uniform. Between times she was busily shopping for a larger house.

President Kennedy had expressed the hope that his Vice-president would help with the entertainment of visiting foreign dignitaries who were being invited to Washington at an unprecedented rate, and the Johnsons' John Citizen house was frankly inadequate. Lady Bird and Lyndon had spent a week in Paris shortly after the election to attend the NATO parliament on behalf of the President, and on their return Bird said: "The time has come when, if I'm ever going to do anything about it, I must look for a bigger house in Washington. We've been talking about it for two years, but when Lyndon and I walked in here with our six suitcases last week and wondered where to set them down, I knew that I really must do something about it."

With a ripple of laughter she added: "Now that it appears we'll have a job in Washington for at least four more years, I guess we should take the step before we spill out onto our doorstep."

The real-estate quest was briefly interrupted while Lyndon and Bird flew to Senegal as the President's official representative for that nation's independence celebration. With her usual zest for doing everything well, she pored over encyclopedias and attended State Department briefings to learn all that she could about the former French colony.

The Johnsons arrived at the glistening white coastal city of Dakar about midnight, and early the next morning Bird asked to visit a peanut farm. Her research had disclosed that Senegal harvests 750,000 tons of them a year, and since peanuts had also grown on her father's plantation, this seemed a good place to begin to understand a friendly new nation.

Our ambassador's wife was startled, to put it mildly. Having scarcely left the capital city herself, she did not expect her guest to be interested in earthy things. Bird went anyway, and inspected the copper buckets of peanuts which had already been harvested. She strolled through grass-hut villages, and stared with fascination at the baobab trees, which produce a gourd-like fruit called monkey bread. Like any American, she was shocked to learn that the trees not only contain an ingredient for cream of tartar but that their hollow, elephantine trunks provide a burial place for poor Senegalese, the wandering griots, who are placed upright inside them at death, to avoid desecrating the land with their lowcaste status.

Tall Lyndon and petite Bird together visited the market places and a trade fair, rubbing elbows and shaking hands so vigorously with the colored masses that they completely blotted the rival Russian delegation from the news.

On their return to the United States, Bird wrote an account of the trip for a Washington newspaper, and in her best journalese began: "Africa is a many splendored continent of bright color and contrast. How can one presume to know anything about a country after three days? Yet, at its hour of independence, Senegal is so breathtakingly brilliant in the array of people, languages, costumes and customs that one tries to absorb it like a sponge."

She also found her dream house. It was the elegant French château, "Les Ormes," which her old friend, Perle Mesta, had decided to sell. The famed hostess, whose tour of duty in Luxemburg inspired the hit musical *Call Me Madam*, had brought decorators and gardeners from Paris to transform the thirty-year-old house into a Washington show place. She had entertained lavishly there in recent years, but some of her pleasure in wining and dining capital officialdom had dimmed with the advent of the Kennedy administration.

Perle had given her enthusiastic all to the Lyndon Johnson candidacy, but when he lost to Mr. Kennedy and then agreed to run on the ticket in second place, "Two-Party Perle" who had started life as a Republican switched political allegiance once again. "I'm still a Democrat," she announced after the Conventions, "but I am for the Nixon-Lodge ticket."

She had even done some campaigning for Republican standard-bearer Richard M. Nixon, and after the Kennedy victory she was definitely out of favor with the new administration in the White House. The Johnsons never forgot her pre-convention support of them, however, but now she was traveling, lecturing, and doing a monthly magazine piece. The big house on the crest of a hill in the fashionable Spring Valley section of Washington had lost its appeal for her, and she decided that an apartment would better serve her needs.

The Johnson performance on the mission to Senegal generated so much good will for America that President Kennedy now tapped Lyndon and Lady Bird for a trip around the world. The administration had been in office less than four months, and with the Cuban invasion fiasco reverberating around the globe, JFK was anxious for LBJ to help improve our damaged image in Asia.

Lyndon had some misgivings about the venture, but he was learning to be a good soldier in the ranks. He therefore deputized a friend to negotiate with Mrs. Mesta on his behalf during their absence, and taking Carl T. Rowan, the first Negro Deputy Assistant Secretary of State of Public Affairs with them, the Johnsons flew off to the Orient.

President Kennedy also dispatched his sister, Jean, and her husband, Stephen Smith, on the same plane and same itinerary, a move which caused a flurry of speculation that JFK did not want his number two man to receive too much personal publicity. The Johnson undertaking, however, was a masterful success with the people. Towering above the shorter Asians, the jovial Vice-president barnstormed his way through crowds exactly as if he were running for sheriff in Austin, petting babies and throwing his arms around ragged natives.

The first stop was war-torn Viet Nam, and Secret Service agents warned the official party to watch what they said to each other inside President Ngo Dinh Diem's Gia Long Palace, because the rooms were bugged. Handsome Madame Ngo Dinh Nhu, the "First Lady" of Viet Nam, whose husband was later to die with his bachelor President brother in a coup d'état, escorted Lady Bird to parliament, where she met the nine women members of the National Assembly.

Bird takes rapid shorthand notes on all of her journeys, and this day she recorded her observation that the tiny Congressional ladies were as lovely as "lotus blossoms." Bird also visited a hospital bulging with wounded soldiers from the battlefront raging nearby, and jotted down a reminder about their "silent baffled eyes." Commenting privately on her reaction to Madame Nhu, who was later to make a head-line tour of America just before the fall of her government, Bird said succinctly: "She's an intense, courageous political personality, but what direction it will take I don't know."

During a visit to Taipai, Bird donned a wide-brimmed, flowered straw hat for a gala ride in a pedicab with Mrs. Chew Cheng, wife of the Vice-president of Formosa.

While in India the Johnsons visited the exquisite Taj Mahal, and when their guide mentioned the perfect acoustics of the tomb, the enthusiastic Vice-president let out a Texas war whoop that startled natives for miles around. The Taj Mahal is a memorial to the love that the seventeenth-century Mogul Emperor Shah Jahan held for his wife who died in childbirth, and Lyndon could not resist kissing Lady Bird while standing in the center of the mausoleum. The State Department had failed to brief him on the fact that public kissing is scandalous to Indians and is therefore forbidden at sacred sites like the Taj Mahal.

Even this could not mar his triumph, however. In neighboring Pakistan, he captured the fancy of the world by greeting a dusty camel driver and inviting him for a visit to the LBJ ranch. Bird frequently maintained a separate schedule from her husband, making the rounds of hospitals and schools in order to double the exposure of their goodwill mission, and the sight of the smiling American lady in her bright red or coral dresses won her a place in foreign hearts.

The Johnsons saw their names in the headlines of newspapers printed in Urdu, Hindi, Chinese, French, and German. Bird sought out the women "doers," who were taking the lead in unshackling their sex in Southeast Asia; and expressed her pleasure that the once downtrodden women were now "putting their hearts and their heads to work, as well as their hands."

In her own quiet way, she was equally as effective as her more flamboyant husband. In the Philippines she had toured Welfareville, the government establishment for deserted children, and laid the cornerstone of a new building for unwed mothers. In Taipeh, she took her turn at sewing machines in the Chinese Women's Anti-Aggression League headquarters, and visited kindergartens and orphanages. She and Jean Smith strolled along the klongs in Thailand on an early morning hand-shaking tour, and made speeches at schools.

Nellie Bly had spent three months circling the globe. Lyndon and Lady Bird returned home in fourteen days, and when friends asked the Second Lady how they had accomplished such a miracle of speed, with so many state visits to distant lands, she laughed and said, "Lyndon wonders why we were so slow!"

They had a joyous reunion with their daughters. Then Lady Bird began to pack again, this time for a major move to the stately white brick house that the Johnsons had purchased from Mrs. Mesta for an undisclosed sum. They also bought some of the furnishings, including the beautiful dining-room set, which seats twenty-two guests, but they promptly changed the name "Les Ormes" to its English equivalent, "The Elms." The Johnsons were determined to give themselves no foreign airs.

The lavish abode on which Mrs. Mesta had spared no expense contained twelve rooms on the first two floors and an office and some storage rooms on the third floor. The office was for Lady Bird, since the Vice-president now had luxurious suites both at the Capitol and in the Executive office building next door to the White House. Lyndon took care of that oversight at home, however, by spreading his office papers all over the king-sized double bed.

Lady Bird remodeled the kitchen to provide more storage space, after securing the usual three bids. The family sometimes felt like tiptoeing across the parquet floors of the formal rooms, which were patterned after those in the palace of Versailles, but they hung their colorful paintings, by such Texas artists as Kelly Fearing and Porfirio Salinas, on the walls.

The terrace room and library soon began to tell the story

of the Vice-president's career in framed photographs and clippings, and Bird arranged her collection of Doughty birds in the recessed shelves of the drawing room.

On the second floor were the gracious master bedroom with adjoining dressing room, the girls' separate bedrooms, a guest room, and a family room. Lucy's private quarters boasted a canopied bed in blue and white, "ruffled and feminine like Lucy," her mother explained to guests.

Lady Bird was receiving fan letters from women throughout the world, but her friends could sense no change in her. Although she was now dining at the White House with visiting heads of state, and traveling widely in presidential planes on good-will missions, she remained as modest and unassuming as the little girl from Karnack had always been.

On business trips to her Austin television station each month, she purchased tourist-class tickets, and when a friend demanded to know why, Tom Taylor's daughter replied matter-of-factly: "Because on planes you get to exactly the same place at the same time. The only difference is that you don't get a drink, and perhaps a little bit of extra service and elbow room, but I have to travel so much that the difference in price is quite a saving. I'm just grateful that they have such a thing as tourist prices."

Lyndon's only noticeable concession to economy was turning off the lights around the house. It amused Bird to see her very generous husband follow along behind his daughters turning off the lights.

"Lyndon really has that light complex to an advanced degree," she chuckles. "I'm sure it's due to the fact that his family had to use kerosene lamps until he was in his teens. He learned as a boy to be saving of light."

She might have added that Lyndon's father used to

waken him before daylight each morning with the perpetual shout "Get a move on, Lyndon; every boy in town's got an hour's headstart on you." Perhaps that is why he has been running ever since.

During her first year as Second Lady, the General Federation of Women's Clubs asked Bird to write an article for its magazine on "Woman's Most Important Role." She began the piece by declaring that the issue had been debated by scientists, politicians, and poets "ever since Eve," but her own view was that women's greatest contributions are "continuity and idealism."

"Historically, most of the great bursts of brilliance have originated with men," she wrote, "but over and over we can see that the continuity and idealism of women have accounted for the improvement of the lot of mankind. I have always felt it is a privilege to be a woman. We give the durability, the determined patience to keep our eyes set on the star of peace for mankind. In our hearts, we have the faith to know that one day we shall find it."

Busy as she was, she continued to take out-of-town friends on sightseeing trips around the capital. Once she remarked that she had now visited Mount Vernon sixty-seven times, "but the most beautiful time of all was the day that it was nearly buried in a snowstorm, and the guide showed us a hole in the door where Martha Washington used to let her cat in and out."

Little Beagle Johnson, the family dog, had moved with them to "The Elms," but he was a roamer who frequently returned to their former house several miles away. One day, Bird was driving herself in her car, when she caught a glimpse of him and stopped to see what he would do. While she watched, he waited sedately at a busy street corner until the light changed to green. When an old lady started across the street, he romped across to the other side with her.

Little Beagle seemed to have learned a lot since the occasion some years before, when he had disappeared from the Johnson's former abode and become the only dog ever listed on the FBI's most-wanted list. That time he was struck by a car, but his name tag provided identification, when a kindly soul took him to a veterinarian.

For several years, Little Beagle held the number two dog license number from the District of Columbia, but when President Kennedy acquired several other dogs besides Charlie, Little Beagle was bumped to fourth place. The endearing little fellow lived until June of 1963, when at the age of fifteen he died of suspected poisoning. He had been an inseparable pal of the Vice-president during his convalescence from the heart attack, and after his death the grieving Johnsons had him cremated. His ashes were then buried on the ranch.

LBJ quickly selected a pair of beagles in Texas from the last litter sired by Little Beagle, to help the family get over Little Beagle's death. The dogs went to Washington with the Johnsons in September, and according to Lucy, "Daddy wouldn't let them put those little puppies in the baggage compartment, so I held one, and he held the other all the way. He kept petting and stroking it, so it wouldn't get scared, and Daddy even slept with the dog on top of him."

Lucy named the new pups Him and Her.

Chapter

12

LADY BIRD'S remarkable adaptability was a godsend to the
Kennedy administration. First Lady Jacqueline Kennedy
had other interests taking priority over politics and
women's meetings, so it was Bird who found the time to
take on such chores.

In their Capitol Hill days, Bird had been accustomed to
taking Lyndon's visiting constituents to lunch and on sightseeing tours. Now America was his constituency, and she
felt that she was "working for all the people." She became
the official ribbon-snipper at flower show openings, cancer
and heart drives, and other charity functions. When foreign
visitors came to Washington, she was pressed into service
to entertain Indira Gandhi, daughter of Indian Prime Minister Nehru, the wives of Prime Ministers, and Empress
Farah of Iran.

During the late summer of 1961, the Vice-president made two emergency trips to Europe, first to the Berlin wall to assure the people of West Germany that we stood solidly behind them, then to Stockholm to attend the funeral of Dag Hammerskjöld, the Secretary General of the United Nations who had died suddenly in a plane crash.

And then came Bashir Ahmed! The marvelously quotable Pakistani camel driver had taken Lyndon's "y-all come see us sometime" seriously. With his usual flair, the Vice-president arranged for the People-to-People exchange program to finance Bashir's air passage, but Lyndon took over from there.

Accompanied by Lady Bird and Liz Carpenter, Lyndon flew to New York to meet the "flying carpet" that was bringing the camel driver to the New World. Word had reached the Johnsons that the wire services were planning to assign their "funniest" writers to the story, but LBJ was not amused. While awaiting his guest's arrival, he telephoned the heads of Associated Press and United Press International and appealed for statesman-like coverage.

"I've been in Southeast Asia," he argued, "and what we need on our side are the camel drivers of the world. The whole world will be watching this reception, and listening to what is said about Bashir. He is my guest, and I think it would be cruel and foolish for us to poke fun at him in print."

Word came that Bashir's plane was running four hours late. The Vice-president was scheduled to make an important speech in San Antonio that afternoon, but nothing seemed more urgent to him than a warm and dignified welcome for his guest. He therefore sent Liz and Lady

Bird ahead to Texas, the former to urge local reporters not to ridicule Bashir in their stories and the latter to pinch-hit for him at the San Antonio political rally for campaigning Henry Gonzalez, the first Texan of Mexican descent to be elected to represent his state in Congress.

Both women did their tasks well. When Liz began to explain that "a lot is at stake" on the Bashir visit, an AP reporter broke in to say that the message had already arrived from New York asking him to respect the Vice-president's wishes. Bird, as usual, was a hit at the rally of six hundred people. Then the two women flew to the ranch, beating Lyndon and his guest there by an hour.

Texans were immediately enchanted by the dignified little man in his knee-length black coat, black astrakhan cap, and flowing white trousers. Lyndon drove him around the ranch in a golf cart, pointed out the country cemetery where his ancestors were buried and the humble cottage where he had been born. It was only a little better than the mud hut in rural Pakistan where Bashir lived with his wife and their six children.

The State Department provided the perfect interpreter in Saed Khan, a former Bengal lancer, and the three men rode horseback across the range, while Bashir delightedly commented that the blooded steed was "smoother than a camel." Watching a filmed TV program of his arrival in New York, the guest exclaimed in astonishment, "How can I be here when I am there?"

Bird and Lyndon were anxious that Bashir not be disturbed by too many press people, so the Vice-president specified that reporters could accompany them only during an inspection tour of the Pedernales River Co-operative, where he would demonstrate how electricity had come within the last forty years to his own arid, dry land, which, like Pakistan, is so short of water.

"I'm not gonna' have reporters at the ranch this trip, though," LBJ firmly told his wife. But at the completion of the electrical plant tour, he telephoned Lady Bird and said, "Honey, I'm bringing these reporters home with us for lunch."

The imperturbable Bird promptly prepared fifteen extra table settings for lunch. She staged a typical LBJ barbecue for Bashir that afternoon, and Lyndon took his guest for a motor-boat ride on the lake. The next day they went to the State Fair in Dallas, and having worried for fear Texans would be shocked to see the camel driver eat food with his fingers, as is the custom with poor people in Pakistan, the Johnsons suggested a lunch that could be managed without knife or fork.

The Fair staff co-operated brilliantly. Each guest, including the Vice-president and all other dignitaries, were handed plates containing a chicken drumstick, stuffed celery, hard-boiled eggs, slivers of carrots, and potato chips. No forks were needed.

Lyndon, already under heavy speaking commitments in the state, said good-bye to his guest the next morning at the ranch, and Liz Carpenter accompanied Bashir to Kansas City for a visit to People-to-People headquarters, a handshake with former President Truman, and an early morning cattle auction. Then they flew to Washington, where the hospitable Lady Bird by now was waiting.

She took Bashir on a special tour of the Capitol, trailed by some fifty reporters, and when she saw his startled expression as they reached the escalator leading down to the subway train, Bird said reassuringly, "You just watch the way I do it, and this will be fun." Very slowly she placed a dainty foot on the escalator; he did likewise; and they descended together.

Bird also escorted Bashir through the White House, where he met President Kennedy, and to the Moslem mosque where the devout Mohammedan exclaimed over the beauty of Islam. They went to a high school in Fairfax, Virginia, and Bashir made such a hit with the students that they collected barrels of books and school supplies which they sent in his honor to Pakistani children.

His delight was unbounded when, besides receiving a free pick-up truck to replace his camel, Bashir returned home by way of Mecca. "Your children are darling," he said to Bird as he shyly told her good-bye, and through the interpreter she replied softly, "Those words sound good in any language."

Lynda and Lucy had meanwhile been having a heady experience of their own. During their parents' absence with Bashir at the ranch, stiff, gold-embossed cards had arrived inviting the two girls to a State Dinner at the White House to be given in honor of President Abboud of the Sudan. Convinced that a mistake had been made, the girls telephoned Mrs. Kennedy to ask if she realized that they were only seventeen and fourteen. Indeed she did, the First Lady replied, and she did want them. She was sure they would enjoy the Shakespeare players, who were making their first White House appearance.

The girls were almost beside themselves at the prospect of such a glamorous evening in grown-up company, but Lady Bird gave them a practical word of caution by telephone: "Read all you can in the encyclopedia about the

Sudan, and don't drink any of the wines at the White House."

Lady Bird seldom worried about the two girls when she was away, because she trusted them implicitly. Convinced that properly trained "twigs" would grow straight and tall, she has never even placed a curfew on their dates. Lynda Bird, in a surprisingly adult comment on her mother's child-rearing philosophy, once observed: "We have moral togetherness. Lucy and I always know that whether Mother is with us or if not, she is thinking of us. Mother has never told us when to be in from a party or date. She just leaves it to our own good judgment. How can you break faith with a woman who does that?"

Lyndon Johnson shares his daughters' admiration for his wife. As he told a friend, Blake Clark: "Bird trusts her children completely, and they know it. She doesn't nag them, but when they seek her advice she sounds like a judge as she weighs all sides. Then she lets them find the answer. I know a lot about mothers. I thought I had the best one in the world, and as a one-time school teacher I've seen a lot of mothers, but I never knew one I thought was more devoted, yet more reserved and less gushy than Bird."

In December of 1961, forty-one women delegates representing thirty-two of the United Nations came down from New York for a meeting with President Kennedy and other officials. Jacqueline Kennedy was away, so Bird not only represented the distaff side of the administration but entertained them with tea at "The Elms." It was almost two weeks until Christmas, but Bird had thoughtfully trimmed two Christmas trees, which flanked the entrance way, and had fastened two wreaths to the imposing double doors. Inside the foyer was another silver-trimmed pine tree, green garlands were draped on the spiral stair rail, and mistletoe festooned the chandelier.

Bird in her own way is as much of a perfectionist as her husband is in his. To help put the distinguished UN women at their ease, she had invited a group of close friends to assist with pinning name tags on the guests, and circulating among them to see that the foreign delegates met the high-ranking American wives and officials.

Each friend was assigned a station, and as soon as the last guest had departed, Bird summoned them into the living room, thanked them, and said: "Now, let's start planning on how the next such party could be improved. I want to hear each of your suggestions."

Bird is aware of the importance of details. Before her first big party for Texans at "The Elms" she met personally with the caterers and each member of the staff to insure that the food and service would leave nothing to be desired.

She introduced a new twist at her ladies' luncheons. Scorning the usual trivia and chitchat of Washington parties, she invited Senate or Cabinet wives to make a talk about some recent experience or trip, so that foreign visitors could discover the vitality of our American way of life.

The Johnsons installed a heated swimming pool at "The Elms," which became a gathering place not only for official dignitaries but for staff members, friends, and the teenage set. Seated beside it one broiling summer day, the Vice-president said: "I've had a lot of disappointments in my lifetime, but never with my family. I've got the best wife and the best two daughters in this world. How Lady Bird can do all the things she does without ever stubbing her toes I'll just never know, 'cause I sure stub mine sometimes."

He plunged into the pool, and swam vigorously up and down its length. Then, shaking the water from his hair, he returned to the conversation: "And our children are so wonderful! I never have any doubt about anything they do, because I have such faith in them, and such respect for their judgment."

Four tragedies marred that first Vice-presidential year for the Johnsons. One occurred only a few weeks after Lyndon took office. At the LBJ ranch for a weekend, they were packed and waiting for the small leased KTBC plane, which frequently took them back and forth to Austin for their flight connection to Washington. As soon as the Austin call came that the plane was on its way, the Johnsons switched on the landing lights of their private airstrip, but they waited in vain. The pilot, who was also their friend, had died in the flaming wreckage of the plane which had crashed against a bleak, fog-shrouded hill nearby.

In November of 1961, Lyndon and Lady Bird were on their way to Phoenix for a dinner celebrating Senator Carl Hayden's fiftieth year in Congress, when their beloved friend, Speaker Sam Rayburn, died. With heavy hearts they attended the anniversary celebration and were planning to fly on to Texas for Mr. Sam's funeral, when a telephone call came for Bird from Sante Fe. Her only surviving brother, Tony, had just suffered a severe heart attack.

Lyndon responded magnificently to the crisis. Like a human dynamo, he personally located his own heart specialist, Dr. Willis Hurst, in Atlanta, and arranged for him to fly immediately to Tony's bedside; he read timetables and scheduled transportation both for the physician and Bird; he arranged to have each of them met at the airport. After attending the Rayburn funeral, he joined Bird in Sante Fe.

Recalling that crisis, the First Lady now says: "Lyndon kept saying, 'you have only one brother,' and all the time he knew my heart was stricken because I would not be able to be present at Sam Rayburn's funeral. But he made the decision, and he just sent me packin'."

It was on this sad occasion that Bird coined the now-famous phrase: "Lyndon's a good man to have around in an emergency."

Dr. Willis Hurst was also a good man to have around, and Tony Taylor eventually recovered, just as Lyndon had done six years before.

The fourth tragedy came at Christmastime. The Johnsons were planning a festive celebration at the ranch, and kinfolks were coming from miles around for yuletide dinner. The Vice-president's youngest sister, Mrs. James Moss of Fredericksburg, had dropped in with her husband for a while on Christmas Eve and was to return the next morning. Lady Bird was stuffing Christmas stockings when the call came that LBJ's forty-nine-year-old sister had just died of a cerebral hemorrhage.

A heavy pall descended on the ranch, and the day after Christmas the Vice-president, his wife, and daughters attended the funeral rites for Mrs. Moss in Johnson City. Lyndon, who "always takes funerals hard," seemed to be having more than his share of them that year.

Chapter

13

THE BRIGHT New Year of 1962 ushered in so much additional foreign travel for the Johnsons that wags began to quip: "JFK wants to keep LBJ out of the country."

Lady Bird's earlier predictions were coming true. Lyndon was indeed making his new job as Vice-president "one of the busiest in the capital." Besides his constitutional chore of presiding over the Senate, the rangy Texan had been given four unprecedented assignments by President Kennedy. He was named Chairman of the President's National Aeronautics and Space Council, which called on him to co-ordinate the United States program for the exploration of space. He was made Chairman of a committee to enforce the prohibition of racial discrimination in hiring by the government and its contractors. He was the number two man on the vital National Security Council, and the Chairman of the advisory committee to the Peace Corps.

To top it all, the President made Lyndon his special representative in diplomatic contacts with nations overseas, with authority to negotiate with them on some levels. It was in this ambassadorial role that Lyndon and Lady Bird traveled that year to Puerto Rico for its tenth anniversary as a commonwealth, to Jamaica for its independence celebration, to five nations of the Middle East, to Italy, and to Puerto Rico again.

The two-week visit to Lebanon, Iran, Turkey, Cyprus, and Greece gave Bird an exciting opportunity to add to the artifacts collection which she had started some years before with a few Indian arrowheads found at the ranch. She visited the sites of ancient excavations, and personally dug with a shovel to unearth broken bits of ancient pottery. These she brought home after she had received permission to do so from the various foreign governments.

Lynda Bird accompanied her parents on this trip. They were intrigued to find that Iran reminded them of West Texas, with its arid stretches, bony hills, and cactus. While LBJ busied himself with affairs of state, Bird and Lynda visited youth camps where young girls had only begun to take off the flowing black veils that had concealed their eager faces from the world around them.

At Ismir, Turkey, which had been Smyrna in biblical times, Bird and her daughter went to a girl's school founded a hundred years before by a group of women missionaries from the Congregational Church in New England. The friendly students pressed around them to report that they took bookmobiles and healthmobiles to remote villages in the Turkish mountains to teach the mothers to read, to boil drinking water for their babies, and to prepare food properly.

The Johnson women were particularly impressed by a town center in Athens, which Queen Frederika of Greece had converted from a walled prison into a play area for children of working mothers. There women could also learn to sew, cook, and use a typewriter. Of the beautiful Greek Queen, Bird said approvingly: "She's a working career Queen."

Neither Lyndon nor Bird were meanwhile neglecting the home front. They gave several receptions for members of Congress, and continued to attend parties given by such close friends as Representative—now Federal Judge—and Mrs. Homer Thornberry, the Eugene Worleys, the Walter Jenkins', and Representative and Mrs. Hale Boggs.

In April, they were hosts at a memorable party at the ranch for the seven Astronauts, who wrote their names in the wet cement of a walkway near the swimming pool. Two days later Bird flew back to Washington, and at a party for the Astronaut's wives told them in her inimitable way: "I think your husbands soon felt just as much at home on the range as in outer space."

Despite the glamor of her new position, Bird was still a politician's wife at heart. She proved it that April when she went to New York as the guest of the Amalgamated Clothing Workers Union and seated herself at a factory machine to sew the first union label on a necktie.

"I'm wearing a hat for Alex Rose and Mr. Potofsky." She smiled roguishly, as she glanced at Amalgamated Clothing President Jacob S. Potofsky. No one had to tell this seasoned political trouper how often the textile workers of America winced at the hatless Kennedy clan. Labor leaders were so enchanted that they made Lady Bird an honorary member of their union.

Political opponents were beginning to refer to the Kennedys as "the royal family," but the nearest thing that the administration actually could claim as "royalty" was Lynda Bird Johnson. The tall, dimpled, brunette beauty had been Texas Duchess at the Yam Festival, before her father became Vice-president, and Queen of the President's Cup Regatta. In 1961, she presided over the International Azalea Festival as its Queen, and the next year she was the Texas Cherry Blossom Princess at the annual celebration in Washington.

Lucy Baines was filling the house with pets, ranging from mice and hamsters to dogs and canaries. All of Lynda's titles seemed incidental to her younger sister, however, when Lucy was selected to present the bowl for the best-dog-in-the-show to a tiny Pomeranian at the National Capital Kennel Club.

Lady Bird's motherly heart opened wide for twenty-year-old arthritic patient Barbara Pace of Jasper, Texas, when she arrived to tour Washington in a wheel chair that summer of 1962. Bird spent the better part of an hour showing the young woman the souvenirs and mementoes in her husband's Vice-presidential office at the Capitol.

That same week, although they had just returned from Puerto Rico, the Johnsons learned that some college exchange students were in Washington before leaving for a month of study at the University of Chile. The Johnsons invited these students for a swim at "The Elms." Later, the Vice-president and Bird sat around the patio with them, and had a songfest to the accompaniment of a student's guitar, while soft drinks, ice cream, and cake were served.

Lady Bird describes that hot afternoon this way: "We

had a freezer of homemade ice cream, and we sat around in the back yard and talked about what they expected to find in Chile, the opinion of America that they expected to leave behind them there, and what they had derived from the corresponding students who had visited their universities."

Eyes sparkling, she continued: "If the day ever came when I didn't feel that I had been refreshed from such exchanges of ideas, and had learned nothing from the students, it would be a sad thing. A cynic is the last person who ought to be in politics."

To explain why she was always so willing to find time for students, she recalled an incident from the time when she had first arrived in Washington as the bride of a Congressional secretary. "A very nice Congressman's wife invited me and several more little secretaries' wives to lunch at the Capitol," she said. "The cherry trees were in bloom, and as we walked across the Capitol lawn we got our picture taken, and it was actually sent home to some of the newspapers. I had the feeling that I had had an intimate glimpse of my capital, and that meant a lot to me.

"Since then, I've been anxious to share my front-row seat in this town with all the people who are responsible for my being here, and also to give a little added pleasure to people from abroad who are trying to understand us."

Lynda and Lucy were not at home on that scorching summer day when Lady Bird and Lyndon entertained the exchange students. Lynda, having graduated from the National Cathedral School for Girls, was at orientation week at the University of Texas, and Lucy was spending the summer at Camp Mystic, winning the M girl "best camper" award.

Not since the Theodore Roosevelt administration a half-century before had small fry and teenagers figured so prominently in the Washington political spotlight. Lyndon made a great hit with Caroline Kennedy, who sometimes rode her tricycle into sessions of the Cabinet and National Security Council. The Vice-president presented the adorable little girl with a two-year-old gelding pony called Tex, and the First Family demonstrated its affection for Lyndon by sending a photograph taken of them with Tex at their rented Virginia estate, Glen Ora. The First Lady autographed the picture: "To dear Lyndon—see how we all love this beautiful Tex. Affectionately, Jackie." Under it, the President in his barely legible scrawl, wrote: "I like the cows, also," since he and Lyndon both had pure-bred Herefords. Some scribblings on the side represented Caroline's signature.

That same fall, Bird was asked to express herself about what the average American woman can do to help win friends for this country aboard. She jotted down a few thoughts, which began: "As a nation, we are incurably hopeful. We feel that people are basically good, and we have made some large bets on that basis. While some critics claim we don't have the long sophisticated view toward diplomacy, I'm glad we've been believers."

She described our foreign aid program as "bread cast upon the waters which, as the Bible says, comes back tenfold in friendship for the United States." She advised Americans preparing to travel abroad to "bone up on all the information about a country," and to take underdevelopment in their stride.

"Growing up in a small cotton town in East Texas," she wrote, "I used an oil lamp until I was nine years old, just as they use in many parts of the world today. I remember what a big day it was when inside plumbing came to Karnack, Texas. When we remember what our country was like fifty years ago, we can better understand how much can be done in just a little tick of time."

She urged that stay-at-home Americans open their homes to foreign students, visitors, and "just plain tourists," and that they organize study groups in order to become "do-it-yourself students" of foreign countries. "My feeling is," she added, "that every American can add to the friendly footprints of his country, even if he never leaves home."

Chapter

14

THE FIRST LADY mischievously describes her husband as "tempestuous and more full of ideas and directions than the rest of us can carry out." Any of his loyal staff members would say amen, but the amazing thing about Lady Bird is that she always meets his deadlines.

One afternoon Bird was relaxing under a hair drier at a beauty salon when she was summoned to the telephone. Her secretary, Bess Abell, reported that a North Carolina patrolman had telephoned from his automobile that the touring Vice-president wanted his wife to join him in North Carolina "within a couple of hours."

Recounting the incident on Mark Evans' television show in the spring of 1963, Bird chuckled: "My secretary was somewhat flabbergasted, but by the skin of my teeth, and with her help, I made it. She got the plane schedule, fished out a dress for me to wear, and arranged for the yardman to pick me up and drive me to the airport. That was the third time I've had a call like that from Lyndon. He goes on these speaking trips, and then when some of our friends ask why he didn't bring Lady Bird along, he suddenly sends for me."

Far from being annoyed by his demanding ways, Bird seems to enjoy them. "If I leave any footprints on the sands of time," she says simply, "it will be because he has been able to achieve something."

She likes to tell about the time they were on their way to a party, and she gave him "about three seconds" to decide which three pieces of legislation he was proudest to have had a hand in while he was in Congress.

Without hesitation, he replied: "I guess the first one was in 1941, when a bill was up in the House to continue the draft. I was one of Sam Rayburn's floor men trying to sell legislators on the importance of continuing it, and it passed by one vote—only three months before Pearl Harbor. The second was the Civil Rights Act of 1957, the first passed in eighty years. The third was the Space Act, which has brought so much in its wake."

In her modest way Bird says: "I sort of like to think that I have one small little bitty chunk in those things, too."

A friend had said of Lady Bird Johnson that "she has the brains of a Scarlett O'Hara and the charm of a Dolly Madison." The nation was by now making this same discovery. The Fashion Group of Philadelphia gave her its "crystal citation" for "her example and influence on women in public life." The Washington Heart Association presented its Distinguished Achievement Award to her, as did the Washington Hebrew Congregation.

The National Association of Colored Women's Clubs

gave her a silver loving cup and a citation in recognition of "her talents as a mother, wife, homemaker, and leader among women." She won the Humanitarian Award from the Ararat Chapter of B'nai B'rith, and citations from Theta Sigma Phi journalism fraternity, from the Volunteers of America, and many others.

Bird was as surprised and pleased as a schoolgirl when she read wire service stories that the Chairman of Indiana's Public Service Commission, in announcing that he was looking for a secretary, specified among the qualifications that she should have "the eyes of Elizabeth Taylor, the poise of Queen Elizabeth, the charm of Lady Bird Johnson, the style of Jackie Kennedy, and the wisdom of Solomon." He added that it would help if the secretary could type and take shorthand. Bird would even have qualified on that score!

For the first time in memory the Second Lady had become Washington's undisputed "top society hostess," just after the First Lady herself. In times past that title had usually been held by such non-official women as the late Evalyn Walsh—Hope Diamond—McLean, Perle Mesta, or Gwendolyn Cafritz.

With the emergence of the New Frontier, Perle Mesta and Gwen Cafritz had gone into eclipse, and a Second Lady for the first time was sufficiently wealthy and talented to wear the unsought crown. Trim, 114-pound Lady Bird not only presided over a Washington mansion, a Texas ranch, a summer home on Lake Wirtz, two adjoining ranch houses which had been converted into guest abodes, and an apartment in Austin; but she also gave such sparkling parties that her invitations were more eagerly sought after than any except those that came from the White House.

Bird had developed a real flair for entertaining. Her press secretary, Elizabeth Carpenter, and her personal secretary, Bess Abell, were also gifted "idea gals," and the Johnson parties began to sparkle with entertainment by Calypso bands, Broadway musical-comedy stars, and Cornball "Country Music" singers. In July of 1961, after Jacqueline Kennedy staged a Versailles-like spectacular at Mount Vernon in honor of the visiting President of Pakistan, Lyndon began to wonder what the Johnsons could provide for his visit to their ranch that would not be too anti-climactic. Bird and Liz came up with an aqua ballet staged by the University of Texas, which was brilliantly performed in the swimming pool while the Pakistani guests dined alongside it.

President Ayub Khan would be the first to say that his weekend visit to the LBJ ranch was anything but an anti-climax to his American visit of state. Although he could not have known this detail of Lady Bird's hospitality, nine cooks were up before dawn to prepare four hundred pounds of beef, two hundred pounds of pork ribs, a hundred and fifty chickens—all for outdoor barbecuing—plus mountains of Texas pinto beans, cole slaw, and sour dough biscuits.

Five hundred Texans had been invited and began arriving at eleven for the one P.M. feast. A Mexican mariachi band strolled from the ranchhouse to the meadow, where long picnic tables with red-and-white-checkered cloths had been set up near the sizzling barbecue pits.

The Johnsons had thoughtfully invited fifty-five Pakistani students from Texas colleges to greet their Chief of State, and every guest, including President Ayub, received a ten-gallon Stetson hat from the Vice-president. LBJ also gave Ayub a hand-tooled Western saddle, a leather-trimmed hunting jacket, a rope, a lasso—and spurs, naturally. Lady Bird presented a set of twelve plates decorated with scenes of historic Texas events to the President for his wife, and cowboy outfits for their three grandchildren.

The evening before, the moonlight was brightened by colorful Japanese lanterns strung from the live oak trees, and sixty prominent Texans had come in by private planes for the aqua-ballet entertainment beside the flood-lighted, kidney-shaped swimming pool. To climax the visit, Lyndon suddenly said to the President of Pakistan, "Let's go see the deer and the antelope play."

With that, the two men drove off into the surrounding hills to watch herds of wild animals grazing on the peaceful slopes. East is East and West is West, but at last the twain had met beside the Pedernales River on LBJ's land.

As soon as her distinguished guests flew home to the Orient, Bird rushed back to pick up the busy threads of her official Washington life. "I don't know how we could get along without Lady Bird," an admiring White House aide once remarked, as she began to pinch-hit not only for Mrs. Kennedy, but for Lyndon and the President as well.

Whenever the First Lady was away on foreign travels or at Hyannis Port and Palm Beach, Bird not only sat opposite President Kennedy at White House dinners and luncheons for official visitors but entertained visitors' wives at "The Elms."

She attended charity benefits, visited hospitals, greeted poster girls and Girl Scouts, sponsored drives, shared recipes, and answered hundreds of letters each week. She described a typical day in this manner: "At nine o'clock I had a Spanish lesson, interrupted to make an appointment for Lynda with the dentist and for Lucy with a geometry tutor; eleven o'clock, I opened the National Cathedral flower show; one o'clock, attended luncheon for the Heart Fund drive and made a little speech; two-thirty to five, I answered mail; five o'clock, entertained thirty-five Peace Corps volunteers; at six, an emergency call had me dispatching Lyndon's tux to the Capitol; then I dressed and joined him at seven forty-five at the White House for dinner."

Admitting that such a rugged pace was "fragmenting," she continued cheerfully: "But the day does come when you see results. You are able to speak Spanish to President Betancourt of Venezuela. Lucy's grades improve. The flower show and the Heart Fund meet their goals, and in the mail comes the letter from an elderly pen-pal: 'Heaven bless you for your recipe for cornbread dressing'!"

Bird kept endless lists of things to be done, and used every moment of her time under hair driers or on airplanes to read reports, sign checks, and make plans for the morrow. With a reminiscent smile, she says: "I often think of that funny old sign on my daddy's store, 'T.J. Taylor, Dealer in Everything.' That's not only the story of my life, but the story of America as well."

Throughout those frenetic three years as Second Lady, Bird so thoroughly compartmentalized her efficient mind that she was able to keep up a steady correspondence with her stepmother and her Texas and Alabama cousins. Bess Abell carefully kept a separate file marked "kinfolks."

Bird also mothered Lyndon's staff, from the eldest to the youngest, and when introducing one of them to a stranger would say with ringing sincerity, "This is one of Lyndon's right arms he can't do without."

Although overshadowed by Jacqueline Kennedy's effective sponsorship of the performing arts, Bird's less publicized cultural activities were also formidable. When the President asked his Cabinet members to buy tickets to the hundred-dollar-a-plate benefit for the National Cultural Center, only the Johnsons and Health, Education and Welfare Secretary Anthony Celebrezze bought a thousand-dollar table each.

Bird sponsored the fund-raising drive for the Arena Stage-in-the-Round, substituted for Jackie at a reception and concert for the National Symphony Orchestra volunteers, gave an after-the-symphony party for Erich Leinsdorf, served as patroness of the Bryn Mawr Alumni Art Auction, and proposed a National Arts and Crafts Center to bring tourist dollars to the United States, improve our native arts and crafts, and provide income for weavers and artisans in silver.

From a private estate sale in Boston the Johnsons bought the first record book of appointments used in the White House by President Abraham Lincoln, and donated it to the White House for perpetual safe keeping.

By the early spring of 1963, Lady Bird's schedule was so back-breaking that she began to wonder if she had been shirking heretofore. On a whirlwind trip on the First of March she went alone to West Virginia; toured projects designed to bolster the state's sagging economy; broke ground for the dedication of a library to be built with Federal funds; toured a plant where out-of-work coal miners were being retrained as painters, welders, and assemblers; presented certificates to the graduates; attended a reception given by the governor; and climaxed the day at a statewide banquet of Democratic women.

The next day she flew to Detroit to join Lyndon at a Jefferson-Jackson day dinner and to meet prominent women leaders. Back in Washington she opened the national flower show, spoke at the Congressional Club, and addressed a luncheon of the Democratic Women's Clubs in Maryland—all in one week.

During that same spring, the incredible Lady Bird hosted a dinner with Lyndon for the King of Laos and his entourage, flew to the Dominican Republic for the Inaugural of President Juan Bosch, gave a reception for the advisory committee of the Peace Corps, presided at the Senate Ladies' Red Cross sessions on Tuesdays, and met with her regular Spanish class.

In mid-March she went to her old "home town" of Marshall, Texas, where she had graduated from high school, to be honored by the Camp Fire Girls. The crowded day began with a morning tea in her honor at nearby Jefferson, then a second tea in Marshall, and a ceremony attended by fifteen hundred Camp Fire Girls and eight hundred members of their families at which she was made an honorary member of the association. Lady Bird brought them a large copper tray from Iran, to be used as a wall decoration in their Camp Fire House, and delivered a warm and revealing speech about her visits to youth organizations around the globe.

She wound up the busy week with a trip to Raleigh, North Carolina, where Lyndon addressed a Democratic dinner, and to Philadelphia, where she spoke at a convention of American Women in Radio and Television, and received an award.

No First or Second Lady except Eleanor Roosevelt had matched Bird's pace.

Chapter

15

LADY BIRD must sometimes have wistfully recalled her early days in Washington when Lyndon and she were bunking down in their one-bedroom apartment. Now she was hostess to the wide, wide world, and sooner or later everyone seemed to turn up at the ranch.

President Truman visited there in the fall of 1959, and President-elect Lopez Mateos of Mexico came the same month. President-elect John F. Kennedy flew down before his Inauguration. German Chancellor Conrad Adenauer arrived in April of 1961, and President Ayub Khan of Pakistan was there three months later.

The reception of four heads of state only began to tell the story of the Johnson's Texas-style hospitality. Newspaper groups came in droves, and while addressing a convention of Theta Sigma Phi members in Texas, Bird issued an impromptu invitation for "y'all to come on over to the home place" and have breakfast with her the next morning. They all came—nearly a hundred of them. Lady Bird accompanied the chattering group of women who had ridden in a chartered bus from San Antonio to the Texas hill country seventy-five miles north on a tour around the ranch.

And what a meal it was! Summoned to breakfast by the ring of a typical ranch triangle, they sat down in the shaded yard to venison sausage, grits, mountains of fresh fruit, homemade peach preserves, and the Johnsons' justly famous buttermilk biscuits. The flags of the United States, Texas, and the LBJ ranch were fluttering from a pole, and on the threshold was a welcome mat, presented earlier to Lyndon by the Women's National Press Club, which reads: "All the world is welcome here."

The mat was inspired by the October, 1961, visit of Bashir Ahmed, the Pakistani camel driver, but his visit was only a sample of many more. Four-H Clubs and school groups descended on the ranch each year, and among the more prominent guests have been fifty United States Senators, thirty delegates to the United Nations, sixteen Ambassadors to the Organization of American States, and the Astronauts.

By the time Lyndon became President, official envoys from more than half the nations of the globe had made the trek to the LBJ ranch for a taste of king-sized hospitality. Mainly they were invited because Lady Bird could not bear to have them think that all of America was like Manhattan or Washington.

After the highly successful visit of the UN delegates, Bird explained in her colorful prose: "We have the real makings of a little United Nations right here on the ranch. Our foreman, Dale Malachek, is of Czech extraction; Alfredo Rodriguez, the ranch hand, is Latin; Alvin Sulte-meier, who drives the tractor, is from Germany; and the cook, Gertrude Jackson, is an American Negro. This is the face of rural America. We have a real goin' concern here, a little UN."

Visitors invariably were shown a picture, hanging in the ranchhouse upper hallway, of the surrender of Santa Anna. The Texans are numbered for identification, and Lyndon's great-great uncle, number 24, is partially ob-scured by a tree. Laughing merrily, Bird explains: "Lyndon is sure they got the numbers mixed up. He says no relative of his would have been behind a tree while pictures were being made."

Despite her multitudinous activities, Bird was by no means neglecting her teenage daughters. Lucy always spent the summers at Camp Mystic in Texas, and one evening as Bird and Lynda were driving home from a visit to the camp, they noticed a red barn converted into a summer playhouse. *Oklahoma* was playing. Both of them love the theater but seldom have the time for it. Without a word, Bird pulled the car off the road, bought two bags of pop-corn and two tickets, "and we sat down utterly lost and oblivious to obligations awaiting at home.

"A lot of our good times together are sort of stolen," Bird says with a smile, "just playing hooky, like that. Lucy feels very special when I go along to superintend her Girl Scout troop on all-day camping trips in the country, or attend meetings at her school. Lyndon enjoys the girls even more now that they're able to discuss grown-up things with him, and I must say that I'm finding their teens—

which I had been warned to dread—the most enjoyable time of all."

Even during her three years as the busiest of Second Ladies, Bird occasionally slipped off to New York with the girls for shows and shopping, and would hop in the car with them for leisurely drives along back roads to enjoy a breath of the country air.

The two girls frequently filled "The Elms" with their own house guests, and Bird treasured every moment filled with girlish giggles. Lynda, the more studious of the two, liked to hold long conversations with her father about history and politics, while Lucy whipped up cookies in the kitchen or played with her pets. Of Lucy, her mother says: "She's pure female, interested in hair styles, in how her dress looks, and the like, but she has a lively, creative mind that may show itself one day in music or writing." Lucy's current passion is science, however, and she envisions herself as a woman in white, working as a technician in heart or cancer research.

Lyndon sometimes smilingly complains that his "three women" gang up on him, but Bird merrily retorts: "It takes three of us to take care of you."

Of their two daughters, Bird muses: "I think they are pretty philosophic, well-grounded youngsters. My own recipe for raising them is to give them a considerable sense of independence, and yet let them know that I trust them a lot and am there to see what comes through."

Pausing judiciously to weigh her thoughts, she adds: "You cast bottles on the water with messages for them, wondering if they'll ever come back. Then, suddenly, the bottles come floating back, and I know that they have learned what I tried to instill in them."

The summer of 1963 was a big moment in all of their lives. Since New Year's Eve of 1961, Lynda had been wearing the Annapolis pin of Navy Ensign Bernard Rosenbach, a young man from Comfort, Texas. In June, when she returned home from her freshman year at the University of Texas, she accepted his ring only a few hours before Bird was giving a home-from-college party for her.

Lyndon had been teasing his daughter about Bernie for sometime, and on a speaking trip to Wisconsin that spring he bought her a painting of a young girl flirting with two sailor boys. Bernie, having just graduated from Annapolis, was now assigned to the destroyer *Jonas Ingram*, which was based on the East coast, and it was President Kennedy's turn to begin kidding Lynda by inventing far-away spots where he was threatening to dispatch the ship.

In July of her last summer as Second Lady, Bird had a few days to think of herself. Lucy was away at camp, Lynda was preoccupied with her friends, and the Vice-president was planning to attend the Governors' Conference in Florida. It seemed a miracle—a week to call her own.

Telling no one but the family of her plans, she flew to Guadalajara with her brother, Antonio Taylor, and his wife, and then set out by car to tour the Mexican byways— Guadalajara, Tiaquepaque, and Ajajic in Jalisco; Pàtzcuaro, Uruapan, and Eurongariquaro in Michoacàn. What an opportunity to practice her hard-learned Spanish conversation! What a joy to be at last where no one knew her or demanded something of her! The reservations were made in the name of her brother, who owns a Mexican arts and crafts shop in Santa Fe, and they had a marvelous time shopping.

Tony Taylor's wife, Matianna, is of Spanish colonial

descent, and since Lady Bird had honeymooned with Lyndon in Mexico more than a quarter-century before, the trio relaxed with happy memories. Once they became gloriously, hopelessly lost on a broken-down road in the middle of the night, and Lady Bird was able to practice her Spanish incognito on a welcome stranger who was still awake.

They pressed on to Mexico City, but by that time reporters had heard enough hints in the countryside to discover her. The wife of President Lopez Mateos, who had been a house guest at the LBJ ranch, gave a dinner for her, as did United States Ambassador Thomas Mann; and at the inevitable press conference, Bird said that she had been on a tour mainly of glass factories and pottery sheds.

"It was delightful," she exclaimed enthusiastically. "The Mexican people are wonderful! So gay, yet at times so sad. And such marvelous craftsmen!"

What a happy summer that was! The Vice-president had confounded the experts—those gentlemen of the press—by settling easily into the difficult role of being seen but not heard, except when President Kennedy wanted him to be. The two men, cautiously at first, had developed tremendous admiration for each other, and JFK patiently but emphatically knocked down recurring rumors that Lyndon would be dropped from the Democratic ticket.

Tall, willowy Lynda was blossoming into a gracious and beguiling image of her mother, and happy-go-lucky little Lucy was developing into a beautiful, wise young lady. Their father proudly said of them: "I will never have to worry about either girl. Lynda Bird is so smart that she will always be able to make a living for herself. Lucy Baines is so appealing and feminine that there will always be some man around wanting to make a living for her."

LBJ used to tease Lucy about the fact that she alone—in a family of tanned, brown-eyed people—had fair skin and vivid blue eyes. He never did so after the occasion in San Francisco when she, only thirteen years old, had spontaneously told a racially mixed audience: "I don't know what to say to you folks. But I often think of my mother who has dark hair and brown eyes. My daddy and sister do, too, while I have light hair, white skin, and blue eyes. But we all get along fine together. If we do, in the same family, why can't everybody, without thinking of the color of people's skin or hair or eyes, or even how they worship God?"

In August, Bird flew with Lyndon to Texas for a couple of speaking engagements. She sat beside her tall husband on the rostrum in Baytown, but as he talked on and on her expression changed from one of wifely admiration to growing concern. She noticed that his voice was growing husky after a long, hard day. He had had no dinner, and he was scheduled for a major speech at a Mayors' Convention in Houston the following morning, before flying to Tennessee to attend the funeral of Senator Estes Kefauver.

Funerals were always an emotional strain for Lyndon, and particularly so, since his own bad heart attack. Now, as Lyndon showed no sign of winding up his address, Bird unobtrusively stepped forward and handed him a note which read: "It's time to stop." As docilely as a lamb, Lyndon wound up his grass-roots oration and took his seat to resounding applause.

Before Lynda had to return to the University of Texas that fall, she accompanied her parents on a good-will mission to Sweden, Finland, Norway, Denmark, and Iceland.

The Johnsons of Johnson City were a hit from the start. While the Vice-president conferred with top-ranking officials, Lady Bird and Lynda toured the farms.

"I was curious," Bird says, "to see how they adjust crops and animals in a land that has twenty-four hours of daylight for three months of the year and six-hour days the rest. How do they manage a tremendous pig production when the animals must be moved indoors on October first and kept in heated barns until April?"

Farm-bred Lady Bird enchanted her Swedish hosts with her expertise about agricultural problems. The Second Lady spent as much time in the barns as in the houses, and when one of the farmers mentioned his work with insemination, Bird delighted him by drawling: "We don't do much about that back at our ranch in Texas, because we sort of want to point at the offspring of our cattle and say, 'See how he resembles his parents.' "

In a ceramics studio, Lynda exclaimed at the sight of a funny, round stone doll: "That is how I will look if I go on eating all this good Swedish food."

That evening at dinner, seated to the right of Prime Minister Erlander in Stockholm, Bird laughed appreciatively when he told her about a misplaced caption beneath a newspaper picture of himself, Senator Hubert Humphrey, and Labor Leader Walter Reuther. The line had read: "Here we have the three leaders of the milita-y junta which has upset the government of Ecuador."

Bird, who admires women of accomplishment, complimented the Prime Minister on the fact that his wife holds down a full-time job teaching arithmetic and science in high school. He responded that teachers are so scarce in Sweden that his wife hoped that by setting such an example it would be difficult for other middle-aged teachers to say they wished to retire.

Finland seemed like a little bit of home. In the first place, the Johnsons were greeted by their old friends, Ambassador to Washington and Madame Richard Rafael Seppala, who had spent a weekend with them at the LBJ ranch. In Helsinki they were honored by the first ticker-tape parade in Finnish history, and it was so reminiscent of campaigning that Lyndon was soon pumping hands in folksy Texas style. To top off the day, the friendly Finns staged a barbecue for the Johnsons in Kaivopuisto.

In the far northern city of Bodo, Norway, the Johnsons spotted a welcoming sign: "North Pole, three hours; LBJ Ranch, thirteen hours and forty-five minutes." Bird, as usual, was making copious shorthand notes, and of Bodo she wrote: "A new phenomenon for me—a completely rebuilt city only nineteen years old. Another monument to the resilience of the human spirit. Germans flattened the town completely when they moved out in 1944. Now every house is new. In defiance of the bitter cold and long winter nights, the houses are bright colored—red, yellow, orange and blue—and window balconies are ablaze with nasturtiums, pansies, calendulas, sweet peas. Town is beyond Arctic Circle. Icy fjords search deep into the loud, busy harbors dotted with ships and rocky islands."

Continuing her notes, she wrote: "Met at airport by large crowd, each of whom arrived on a bicycle, and when our small caravan of cars started into town I felt like it was a parade of the Pied Piper of Hamelin, except that our followers were all on bikes. What interested me most was the picture of how man can react to disaster by completely rebuilding an enchanting town."

In Denmark, while Lyndon utilized Sunday to rest and work on new speeches, Bird and Lynda toured model farms. That evening the Johnsons visited the Tivoli, and flowers were strewn along their route. As Lyndon spontaneously left the car to march on foot behind the Tivoli Guard, the friendly crowds began rhythmically clapping their hands in time to the music of the band.

Prime Minister Jens Otto Krag presented the Vice-president with a chair made of palisander and black hide, and when Lyndon seated himself in it, Krag approached him with the next gift he had been holding behind his back. It was a stone-age ax made of flint some 4,500 years ago, and Danish photographers wailed that they had missed the "picture of a lifetime"—their leader stealing up on the United States Vice-president with a concealed weapon in his hand.

Despite the harsher climate, much of Scandinavia reminded Bird of her own childhood days on the plantation. On a tiny island off the coast of Finland, the eight-year-old daughter of the Finnish Ambassador led her through forest trails to show where she went each day to collect the milk. The little girl told Bird that the woods are fairy-like and filled with trolls and elves, both good and bad. Lady Bird, having been reared by an unworldly woman who also took her for long strolls in the woods, knew exactly what was meant. This was the first good-will visit that a United States President or Vice-president had ever paid to Scandinavia, and it was a stunning success.

Back home in Washington, Lucy Baines had been having a minor triumph of her own. Left behind under the chaperonage of Willie Day Taylor, the Vice-president's long-time secretary, she modeled three different costumes in a fashion show staged at the Congressional Club. More than 850 guests attended, and sixteen-year-old Lucy seemed so poised that someone asked whether she had done modeling before.

Winsome little Lucy replied in her most grown-up manner: "I did some modeling a long time ago, when I was quite young, but this was my first really big fashion show."

The Second Family was making fashion news all over. Lyndon displaced Senator Barry Goldwater on the Fashion Foundation of America's list as the best-dressed man in public life, and *Diplomat Magazine* picked Lady Bird as the best-hatted woman in the land.

Bird, meanwhile, had emerged unscathed from her first critical assault in the press. Having accepted the honorary chairmanship of the Independence Ball honoring Israel's Fifteenth anniversary, she was astounded by a blast from Najdat Fathi Safwat, Chargé d'Affaires of Iraq, who not only wrote a letter of protest to her, but to letter-to-the-editor columns in newspapers as well.

The Iraqi envoy, charging that "the State of Israel is based upon the usurping of another nation's land by force," urged Bird to withdraw her name from "such a celebration" and added: "I beseech you to uphold the beautiful image we have of you, an image representing kindness and justice and equality."

Bird replied with quiet dignity that the easiest course for the wife of a public official would be never to lend her "name, hand, or heart to any charitable or commemorative endeavor," and that his letter made such a procedure tempting. She added, however, that she tried to be "accessible and available to as many as possible, without distinction as to religion, race, or region." Interestingly enough, it was Republican Senator Hugh Scott of Pennsylvania who first rose to the defense of "the lovely lady of the Vice-president," and questioned the propriety of the Iraqi action. Bird stuck to her guns.

Lynda Bird returned to college in late September, dreaming of becoming a June bride. With both girls back in school, the foremost thought in Bird's ever-practical mind was to do all that she could to further the re-election of the Kennedy-Johnson ticket in 1964. Off to a running start before New York's GOP Governor Nelson Rockefeller had even thrown his hat in the Presidential ring, Lyndon and Lady Bird hit the whistle stops of three New England states.

Bird frequently maintained a separate schedule of her own, to increase political exposure, but both Johnsons attended a hundred-dollar-a-plate re-election campaign dinner in Connecticut for Senator Thomas Dodd, a dinner which raised a war chest of seventy-five thousand dollars.

The Second Lady returned home only long enough to repack her suitcase and give a large dinner party for Lucy Baines that evening. Early the next morning she flew off to California alone for two days of Democratic women's rallies. At a Democratic Ladies' Luncheon in San Francisco on October twenty-eighth, she enchanted her audience with a chat about her busy life as the wife of a top official.

Her wit bubbled through when she told how Lynda "stopped her father cold" in Athens with this line: "As Mother was saying when she spoke at the Acropolis today . . ."

Bird described the glamorous dinners for André Malraux, and for the Nobel prize winners at the White House.

She mentioned her thrill at awarding scholarships on behalf of the President to three blind students who had graduated with honors.

"White House dinners are always a choice invitation," the future First Lady said. "To me it is always a great thrill to walk into that stately gold-and-white dining room, see the brooding picture of Lincoln looking down sternly from the mantlepiece, and read the prayerful quotation [on the mantle] from John Adams in 1800: 'I pray heaven to bestow the best of blessings on this house and on all that shall hereafter inhabit it. May none but honest and wise men ever rule under this roof.' "

Bird talked about the visitors to the LBJ ranch, which is in a part of Texas that was partly settled by a wagon train of 120 German families in the 1840's. "Their descendants still speak German," she said, "and the delightful German Chancellor, Mr. Adenauer, was greatly surprised to be greeted at a Texas barbecue in German by hundreds of men, women, and children.

She recalled the colorful entourage of Pakastani President Ayub Khan, and the "exotic sight" of the Pakistani ladies in their graceful saris strolling along the Pedernales River. One of her most enjoyable evenings in a lifetime, she said, was driving her sari clad guests through the rolling hills to see the deer, and trying to "match tall tales" with them. "We had some Texas rattlesnake stories to tell," she laughed, "but nothing to equal their tales of boa constrictors in Pakistan."

That was just the frosting on the cake, however. Bird then launched into a sales talk on what Democratic women should do to prepare a "victory plan" and help raise a 1964 television fund for the campaign.

Back in Washington for three breathless days, Bird attended two State Department briefings on the European Common Market. Then she repacked her suitcases and departed with Lyndon for a week's tour of the Benelux countries. On the day of her return, she entertained twenty-five wives of Cabinet officers and other top officials, mapping feminine strategy for President Kennedy's re-election campaign; and then she made a frontal attack on her piled-high desk.

In only ten days they were going to Texas with President Kennedy for a series of Lone Star State events. She would have to get to work immediately on her Thanksgiving plans at the ranch for the week afterward.

I had a long interview with Lady Bird a few days before she flew to Texas on that last tragic trip of the President's. By this time she had traveled 120,000 miles to thirty foreign countries at the side of the Vice-president, and had seemingly loved every moment of the wearisome schedule. I asked if she enjoyed her role as Second Lady, and she replied with an impish grin: "I'd be a vegetable if I didn't! I have an omnivorous curiosity about the wide, wide world, and Lyndon's position has given me an unparalled opportunity to be exposed to it both at home and abroad. My life is a wonderful kaleidoscope of interesting things. The best part is being exposed to what's going on in the world today. It's really quite marvelous to sit next to the Prime Minister of Holland and hear him discuss the Common Market, or next to the Shah of Iran while he describes the damming of a great river in his arid land.

"I love to see America, too," she continued breathlessly. "I see the faces of America spread out before me as I travel through the land, and I never tire of it."

She conceded that her multitudinous governmental duties often interfered with her household chores. "Every time I get back to the ranch I sigh at the way the closets are," she mused, "but when there's sometimes a two-week lull in the summer, I sort of get caught up on things and see that the peach preserves get put up."

Bird confided that she was looking forward to the Thanksgiving weekend, when she and Lyndon were planning to go deer shooting, and to the longer holiday at Christmastime. "I want Christmas to be especially festive this year," she bubbled, "because we don't know how much longer we'll have both girls with us. After all, Lynda Bird is nineteen, and very much in love. She and her young man hope to be married next summer. Who knows where she may be next year? That's why I'm inviting all the kinfolks for Christmas at the ranch this year, to make it extra special."

Chapter

16

HOSPITABLE Lady Bird Johnson was in unusually high
spirits as she set off for Texas in the third week of November, 1963. During the Presidential campaign three years
before, she had sturdily criss-crossed her home state alone
or with the Kennedy sisters and sisters-in-law in tow.

Jacqueline Kennedy had missed the warmth of that
Texas reception because she was pregnant with little John-
John, but now the beauteous First Lady would personally
sample the greatness and magic of the Second Lady's
beloved home state. Bird was proud and pleased that the
lovely young woman had chosen Texas as the first place
to which she would accompany the President on a campaign trip since she had moved to the White House.

Speeches by President Kennedy and his Vice-president
were scheduled for Houston, Fort Worth, Dallas, and

Austin; but after the last words had been said on November twenty-second, the President and Mrs. Kennedy were to be overnight guests of the Johnsons at their famed ranch. The President had visited there once before—while he was the President-elect—but it would be a new experience for Jackie.

With their usual thoughtfulness, Lyndon and Bird had arranged that the latter's favorite Tennessee Walking Horse, then undergoing training in Tennessee, would be returned to the ranch in time for the First Lady's visit, for she loved to ride.

Cactus Pryor, the homey master of ceremonies at KTBC, was bringing Texas talent to the ranch, and among the other entertainment acts planned for the Kennedy visit were quarter-horse cutting, whip cracking, and sheep-herding demonstrations.

The loyal ranch staff had been up since dawn baking quantities of pies, which were already cooling in the big country kitchen, while the Presidential parade rolled along the streets of Dallas toward Mr. Kennedy's date with destiny. The colorful crowds lining the streets were friendly and enthusiastic. How relieved Bird was—for she could not forget the spitting, shoving mob that had surrounded Lyndon and herself on that bleak day near the close of the 1960 campaign. Only a week before, United Nations Ambassador Adlai Stevenson had been the object of abuse in this city where shy, gentle Lady Bird had attended junior college. It had nearly broken her heart to think that a small segment of people in this city she had loved as a girl could behave so boorishly. But today—today everything was all that the heart could desire.

Seated in the third car of the Presidential caravan between her tall, smiling husband and Senator Ralph W. Yarborough of Texas, Bird felt an encirclement of love radiating out from the jubilantly waving Texans who lined the streets until the terrible sounds of shots rang out.

A few weeks after that horrifying day, the new First Lady and I sat talking in her bedroom on the second floor of the White House. The first cruel shock had passed, but grief simmered just below the surface of her luminous dark eyes as Bird described her impressions of the tragic event that had cast her husband into the Presidential role. These are the words she spoke: "The air was bright and clear and beautiful. It was a gorgeous day, and we were in a gala mood because of this wonderful reception. It was a feeling of relief, too, because I think all of us had reached the point of relaxation, after our earlier worries about how the political context of the day would go, and what sort of reception we would get in Dallas.

"I had never thought that there would be anything worse than a hurled tomato or egg, or an ugly sign, but suddenly in that brilliant sunshine there was a sharp rifle shot. It came, I thought, from over my right shoulder and above. A moment passed, and then there were two more in rapid succession.

"I could see in almost the same instant that everybody in the lead car went down. Rufus Youngblood, the Secret Service man who was in the front seat of our car, simply vaulted across to the back. I don't see how he got over in that crowded space, but he fell on top of Lyndon and pushed him to the floor. Mr. Youngblood is the politest of men, but he just said to Senator Yarborough and me, in a preëmptory voice, 'Get down.'

"Yarborough and I did the only thing we could in that

[164]

limited space, which was to stoop our heads forward. The car speeded up to a terrific pace, as I heard the radio connection say, 'Let's get out of here.' I thought about the books—*It Can't Happen Here*, and *Seven Days in May*—but your mind refuses to accept such things. For the first second I had thought it was a firecracker. I couldn't believe what it was.

"The speed of our car was almost frightening. Then the brakes slammed on, the cars began to swerve to the left and whirl into a driveway, and it was only when I looked up and saw it was a hospital that I realized this was bad. Yarborough said over and over, 'Oh, my God, have they shot the President?' I said, 'No, I don't think that can be.'

"Then we ground to a halt in front of the hospital, and as I looked up into the lead car, I saw sort of a drift of pink—like pink blossoms—lying across the back seat. I suppose it was Mrs. Kennedy in her pink suit, actually lying on the President.

"The Secret Service men, one on each side, hustled us through the hospital door, and right, left, right, left. I couldn't have retraced my steps if I had tried. We wound up in a little room about eight-feet square, whose walls were lined with sheets, and there we stayed while Secret Service men came and went for quite a long while. Others were also coming and going, too, and you tried to read on each face the message it conveyed."

Lady Bird paused to struggle briefly with her emotions. Then, in her beautifully self-contained manner, she continued with the sad recital: "I went to see Mrs. Kennedy during this agonizing period, and I found her quite alone in the hall, right outside the room where I suppose the President was. I never wanted to comfort anybody so much in my life, and I never felt so mute and helpless. I don't know what it is—whether it's a combination of great breeding, or great character, or great discipline—that enabled her to be so calm. She was utterly calm, but when you looked at her eyes you could almost die!"

I asked if she put her arms around the sorrowing First Lady, and Bird replied quietly: "Just that! Then I told her how much I wished that I could help. I didn't know definitely that the President was gone, but I knew that it was desperate. Mrs. Kennedy murmured sweet little things to me—nothing that I can recall—but I think she knew how hard I was trying. We both knew that we were trying."

Bird then saw her beloved friend, Nellie Connally, whose husband had also been wounded while he rode in the lead car with President Kennedy. "With Nellie it was quite different," Bird said softly, "because, you see, Nellie and I have been through many, many tragedies together, as well as some happy days. Nellie is one of these chin-out, fresh-spoken, fightin' young women, and we just hugged and kissed and prayed and cried together. With Nellie it was possible to do that, because we were such close, dear friends."

Bird returned to the little room where Lyndon waited with the Secret Service guard. The youthful, gallant young President had lost his fight for life, and Lady Bird sensed, when she saw the face of Kenneth O'Donnell, JFK's intimate friend and advisor, what the sad verdict would be.

"I suppose the first time I really knew, however, was when someone came into our little room and addressed Lyndon as 'Mr. President.' I don't even recall who it was."

[Actually, it was Assistant Press Secretary Malcolm Kilduff.]

I asked Bird to describe the subsequent events at the plane that was to take their party back to Washington. She continued: "There were several calls made to Washington about the swearing-in and where it should take place. It was on the advice of the Attorney General [the assassinated President's brother, Robert Kennedy] that it took place on the airfield in the plane. Judge Sarah Hughes arrived to administer the oath. She had been with us in every campaign since 1941, sometimes when the going was rough. She was an old and loyal friend, but she is also a highly capable woman."

And what were Lady Bird's feelings as she stood on one side of her husband, with Jacqueline Kennedy on the other, while he swore the Presidential oath?

Bird thought a moment, and then replied softly: "I felt that I was stalking across the stage in a Greek tragedy; just putting one foot before the other. There was a sense of unreality and nightmare and great tragedy; yet there was also a sense of wanting to take in, and remember, everything that was going on. It was a state of intense aliveness; yet of intense cessation of the normal processes.

"That doesn't adequately describe it. I only remember an infinite compassion for Lyndon, that's all. Then I sat down, and each person was wrapped in his own thoughts. I think someone served us hot bouillon, or perhaps it was coffee, and the plane was off the ground within seven minutes after the swearing-in."

Grieving, soul-searching Lady Bird Johnson was now the First Lady, and a new chapter in her life had begun.

[167]

Chapter

17

A STUNNED nation huddled before its television sets to watch the landing of the Presidential plane in Washington. A delegation of sober-visaged Congressmen stepped forward to meet the new President and his lady, while at the other side of the big jet Attorney General Robert Kennedy assisted his brother's widow to alight. Her pink suit, which she had donned with care that morning in Dallas, was now streaked with her husband's blood.

White House aides helped to lift the coffin of their fallen chief into a waiting ambulance sent from the Bethesda Naval Hospital. Jacqueline and Bobby slipped in beside the coffin, and the ambulance swept away from public view. They were alone with their grief.

A corps of Secret Service agents surrounded the Presidential car as it rolled through the dark streets of Washington to "The Elms." Bird was soon to learn with pride that her daughters had conducted themselves extremely well.

Lynda Bird, on first hearing the news of the assassination at her university classes, went immediately to the Governor's mansion in Austin to comfort the children of Governor Connally, who lay wounded in a Dallas hospital. Lynda knew the children needed a friend close by, since their mother was still at the hospital with their father.

Lucy Baines, called from her junior class at the National Cathedral School for Girls in Washington, was told of the tragedy by Headmistress Katherine Lee. Lucy then attended the special religious services hastily arranged in the school gymnasium, after which she went home to await her parents' return. "Scooter" Miller rushed to "The Elms" to be with Lucy, and found her washing her hair. Trying to control her tears, the sixteen-year-old girl explained: "Daddy will want me to look nice, and my hair was a mess. He always says to me, 'Lucy, comb your hair and put on some lipstick.' I can't let him down now."

Early the next morning, Bess Abell arrived at "The Elms" after only one hour's sleep. Lady Bird's personal secretary had been at the LBJ ranch overseeing preparations for the Kennedy visit, and when word came of the President's assassination she flew immediately to Dallas, then on to Washington, arriving at 6:00 A.M.

Bird, who was conferring with the staff at "The Elms," looked up at sight of her secretary and exclaimed: "Oh, poor, poor Bess. You've just had no sleep at all!" It was like the First Lady to worry about everyone except herself, after having just been through the most grueling day of her life.

[169]

A little later she telephoned Nellie Connally to ask about the Governor's progress, and to commiserate with her. When Nellie, in turn, asked about Lyndon, Bird replied: "Oh, he's just wonderful. He's staying up later, and getting up earlier, and thinking of everything before the rest of us do."

The next few days were the saddest of Bird's life. Tenderhearted and motherly, she yearned to find some way to comfort Mrs. Kennedy, the other members of the Kennedy family, and Lyndon. Lynda Bird flew home from Texas to ease her mother's burden. Mail descended in bulging sack loads, and some of the Senate wives as well as other friends came to "The Elms" to help with the mail and the telephones.

Heads of state began to arrive from every part of the world, and the living had no time for the luxury of grieving in private. Although President Kennedy's office had been cleared of all personal mementoes by his heartbroken staff, President Johnson attacked his multitudinous new tasks from his old office suite in the executive office building next door to the White House. He had no wish to disturb Mrs. Kennedy.

The pageantry of the funeral, which fulfilled every request of Jacqueline Kennedy's, was unequaled in American history. Lady Bird rode beside her husband in the hushed cortege from the Capitol to the White House, and then walked with him from the White House to St. Matthew's Cathedral six blocks away. Before them strode the black-gowned Jacqueline, magnificently courageous. Behind them came aged President Charles de Gaulle of France, King Haile Selassi of Ethiopia, Prince Philip of Britain, and scores of other dignitaries from foreign lands.

Following the funeral, the cortege slowly wended its way to Arlington Cemetery, where other fallen heroes of America's wars lay. The new First Family formed a dark cluster against the bright backdrop of historic Robert E. Lee Mansion, while the widow lighted the eternal flame beside her husband's grave and taps sobbingly reechoed through the surrounding hills.

It was a day to test the endurance of the sturdiest of people and to try men's souls, but it was not yet ended. After Mrs. Kennedy had valiantly greeted the official visitors from afar, Lyndon received an unprecedented parade of Kings, Presidents, Potentates, and Prime Ministers at the State Department. This was to have been an all-male reception, and Lady Bird was just sitting down to a late lunch at four P.M. at "The Elms," when the telephone rang.

It was Chief of Protocol Angier Biddle Duke, conveying the new President's request that Bird come down and join him "to help with the lady visitors." Leaving her lunch untouched, the black-clad wife of the new President rushed down to stand beside her husband in a somber receiving line. While the towering President bent over to listen to the hushed words of the world's leaders, Lady Bird found soothing things to say to Queen Frederika of Greece, Madam Pandit of India, and Foreign Minister Golda Meyer of Israel.

She also spoke glowingly of Jacqueline Kennedy, whose exquisite poise throughout the long ordeal had reminded Bird of a line from President Kennedy's Pulitzer prize-winning *Profiles in Courage*. She quoted it softly: "The most admired of human virtues is courage, which is grace under pressure."

Those words could also have described Lady Bird Johnson.

The day after the funeral, Mrs. Kennedy sent head White House Usher J.B. West to "The Elms" to brief her successor on the housekeeping problems of the executive mansion. He brought with him a blueprint of the shining edifice which was rebuilt, except for the outer walls, during the Truman Administration. Even before his arrival, however, Lady Bird had announced that her move to the White House would depend entirely on the wishes and desires of Jacqueline Kennedy.

"I wish to heaven I could serve Mrs. Kennedy's happiness," she said in a statement. "I can at least serve her convenience. I have had considerable experience in innumerable moves of children, pets and household things, and I know what moving involves. It is only when the last chore she wishes to do is done that I will contemplate moving."

The late President's widow invited Bird to the White House for a private tour of the family quarters, so that she could decide which rooms would require refurnishing. Some of the furniture there belonged to the Kennedys, and would be placed in storage until Jackie found a new home for herself and the children. Then the two women went downstairs to the East Room to hear an address by President Johnson to Latin American members of the Alliance for Progress.

Mrs. Kennedy expressed the hope that Caroline's school, with its enrollment of twenty-one five- and six-year-old youngsters, could continue to meet on the White House third floor until the Christmas holidays. The Johnsons were in heart-felt agreement; and President Johnson interrupted his heavy schedule of appointments to visit the classrooms and greet each child in person. So also did Bird.

The next day Mrs. Kennedy flew with Caroline and John-John to Hyannis Port to spend the Thanksgiving weekend in the Kennedy compound with other members of the bereaved family. The Johnsons, who had once anticipated a relaxing holiday at the ranch, swimming and deer-hunting, remained at "The Elms." The new President was spending eighteen-hour days at his desk.

While Lyndon wrestled with the problems of a government in transition, and urged every member of the Executive Branch to continue on in his Administration, Bird took steps to allay any possible suggestion of conflict of interest. Three days after the funeral, she filed application with the Federal Communications Commission requesting permission to transfer all of her broadcasting properties to a trusteeship.

The vast holdings, now worth several million dollars, which she had nurtured from a $21,000 original investment, were to be administered hereafter by A.W. Moursund of Johnson City and J.W. Bullion of Dallas. The arrangement stressed that the Johnsons were to be informed of no decisions made by the two trustees, and that control would remain with them as long as Lyndon B. Johnson held Federal office.

At the close of the Thanksgiving weekend, as Lynda Bird prepared to return to the University of Texas, Bird's frugality re-asserted itself. Kissing her eldest daughter good-bye, Bird reminded her that "you are loved," and said that they would continue to talk each evening by telephone, just as they had always done.

In a shocked voice Lynda exclaimed: "But Mother, you

[173]

can't call the White House station-to-station." It would cost more now.

With over twenty thousand other students, Lynda resumed attendance at her classes, but there was a difference. Everywhere that she went, Secret Service agents now accompanied her, even to her classes in English, Latin, history, government, chemistry, and the Bible.

"Here comes the brigade," she would say as she stepped from her dormitory door flanked by Secret Service agents, to discover reporters and photographers awaiting her. She dressed as she always had, in sweaters and skirts, black loafers and white socks; but after a week of facing shutter-clicking cameras, she telephoned to ask Lady Bird how much longer the photographers would be around. "I'm running out of clothes," she explained.

Her close friends noted with relief that Lynda remained unaffected by her father's exalted new position. They observed, too, that she was still wearing the engagement ring from Bernard Rosenbach, who had spent the Thanksgiving holidays with the Johnsons at "The Elms." But they knew that Lynda was now under heavy pressure to transfer to a university in the Washington area at mid-term. Not only would it be easier for the Secret Service to guard her when she was living at the White House but her mother frankly needed the radiant, dimpled young daughter who gave her such joy.

Lucy Baines was also taking her changed life in stride. Although the headmistress had phoned "The Elms" to say that Lucy need not come back to school the day after President Kennedy's funeral, she arrived at noon with bulging grocery sacks to deliver her share of the food for the school's Thanksgiving boxes, and stayed for the rest of her classes.

The next day she and Lynda accompanied their mother to the familiar United States Capitol, and seated themselves quietly beside Bird in the "family gallery" to hear their father's first Presidential address to a joint session of Congress. His speech, by the unanimous agreement of all who listened, was the finest he had ever made. Afterward, as he strode up the center aisle amid the sound of a standing ovation from his former colleagues, he paused halfway and looked for a few seconds at his "three womenfolks" in the front row of the balcony. Bird lovingly but unsmilingly returned his gaze, and Lynda lifted her chin in a gesture that told him she was proud. He then left the chamber, with the echo of thirty-two separate bursts of applause still ringing in his ears.

Talking with Congressional leaders privately, after her husband's stirring address, Lady Bird said proudly: "Lyndon's going to give this all he's got. It was an anguished spot for him to be in, but the speech was great, and I have great faith in him."

Exactly two weeks after the assassination of President Kennedy, Mrs. Kennedy moved from the White House to an historic Georgetown house lent to her by Undersecretary of State Averell Harriman. Before doing so, she stood behind a screen while President Johnson awarded the Presidential Medal of Freedom to thirty-one persons whom his predecessor had designated for the award. Then, after a hushed moment, he made two surprise awards posthumously to President Kennedy and Pope John.

Lady Bird took to her heart the three women recipients of the nation's highest peacetime award. To Miss Genevieve Caulfield, the blind teacher of the blind in Southeast Asia, Bird recalled their meeting at a school in Bangkok in 1961. In talking with Mrs. Annie Dodge Wauneka, health worker among the Navajo Indians in Arizona, Bird discovered, as she often did, that they had mutual friends, including Bird's brother, Tony, in Sante Fe.

She greeted Marian Anderson as the old friend that she is. They had last shared a platform in Connecticut the month before at a dinner honoring Senator Thomas Dodd, and, earlier, the Negro singer had visited the Johnsons at the LBJ ranch following a singing engagement in Texas.

Bird attended the State Department luncheon hosted by the Secretary of State and Mrs. Rusk for the Medal of Freedom winners, and in reflecting on the occasion observed: "It was actually magnificent. I felt that I had seen a gathering of an Olympian conclave of people. It was like a kaleidoscope of the brains and the talent and the heart of this country."

That afternoon Bird paid tribute to her predecessor on a filmed television show. "Jacqueline Bouvier Kennedy," she began, "leaves a shining gift of beauty in this historic house. At every turn we are freshly conscious of our heritage. The most knowledgeable expert, as well as the bus loads of school children who visit, will always know that a young and radiant First Lady lived here. We know her better than ever before, and hold her close to our hearts with inexpressible pride."

Then Bird returned to her packing and her mail, for the next day was moving day for the Johnsons. The President began it with a brisk morning walk around his old neighborhood, while vans backed up to the stately door of "The Elms." Bird spent the day scurrying through the rooms of the lovely house that she had now listed for sale. In mid-afternoon she personally carried a treasured portrait of the late Speaker, Sam Rayburn, into the Executive Mansion, and hung it on a wall in the family sitting room at the end of the second-floor hall.

It was a Saturday. Lucy had gone to school that morning in response to a notice advising students that they would be paid $1.25 an hour to lick envelopes. Later, as her mother rolled out of the driveway of "The Elms" in a White House limousine, Lucy followed in the white convertible Corvair that her father had given her for her sixteenth birthday shortly before. With Lucy were her beloved beagles, Him and Her. With Bird were her press secretary and staff director, Elizabeth Carpenter, and her social secretary, Bess Abell. Both women had been on the Johnson staff since the early Vice-presidential days, but now they had become the first official appointees of the new Administration. Moving day was almost over.

The Johnsons of Texas slept in the White House for the first time that night of December seventh. Their many admirers fervently began to hope that there was no truth to the old adage about moving days: "Saturday flit, short sit."

Lady Bird Johnson, perhaps the most experienced chatelaine ever to become First Lady, now presided over a yearly household budget of $670,000, and a domestic and maintenance staff numbering seventy-five. In addition to the maitre d'hotel, two housekeepers, four butlers, six cooks, a valet, five doormen, five housemen, a head laundress, a pantry woman, and eight maids, the Johnsons took along their own domestic staff: Mrs. Zephyr Wright, the Negro cook who had been with them since two years before Lynda was born; Mrs. Helen Williams, the children's long-time nursemaid and housekeeper; and Mrs. Lee Gregg.

Zephyr would reign supreme in the family kitchen which the Kennedys had installed on the second floor in the northwest corner that had once been Margaret Truman's girlhood bedroom. When the Kennedy Administration began, Congress had provided an extra hundred thousand dollars for redecoration of the family quarters, but practical Bird decided to use the rooms much as she found them. Workmen merely patched the holes and painted where the previous occupant's pictures and paintings had hung on the off-white walls.

For the second time in history America had a President named Johnson. Each had assumed that office on the assassination of his predecessor: Andrew Johnson on the death of Abraham Lincoln and Lyndon Johnson on the death of John Fitzgerald Kennedy.

LBJ reminded family friends that the earlier Mrs. Johnson was called Eliza, as was his own grandmother. Interestingly, Lady Bird could point to another President who also bore her Taylor family name—Zachary Taylor.

There the resemblance fortunately ended. Both Eliza Johnson and Margaret Mackall Smith Taylor had been invalids as First Ladies, and their married daughters took over the management of the White House. Although Lady Bird Taylor Johnson was, like them, of Southern heritage, she was no languishing Southern belle who dreamed of magnolias and Dixie moonlight. The new First Lady is a "doer," a woman whom her press secretary describes as "a touch of velvet with the stamina of steel."

A new era was dawning at 1600 Pennsylvania Avenue. The folksy, warmhearted Johnsons of Texas were now the First Family indeed.

Chapter

18

It SCARCELY seemed like the Christmas season, that year of 1963. Flags flew at half-mast from every government building and along embassy row. The interior of the White House, into which the Johnsons had moved, was draped with black crepe; and Bird herself wore mourning black. Congress was still sitting, in the longest peacetime session of history, and the new President was also breaking records with the number of his appointments.

On December the eleventh, Lady Bird pinch-hit the final time for her beautiful young predecessor. Jacqueline Kennedy had planned to distribute Christmas gifts to little patients in the Children's Wing of D.C. General Hospital. After her husband's assassination, she asked if the new First Lady would serve in her stead.

Accompanied by Lucy Baines, Bird made the rounds of

the wards, taking remembrances of Jackie wherever she went. "I want you-all to know that Mrs. Kennedy was looking forward to seeing you today," she constantly repeated as she handed out toys. "I'm just her substitute." To a convalescing boy, age ten, she said brightly as she gave him a truck and a tank: "They look real steady, don't they?" She presented a little girl with a jigsaw puzzle saying: "That's a hard one, but I bet you can do it."

The First Lady spent an hour going from room to room, dipping into large baskets tied with red ribbons for the right gift to match the age and sex of each child. For those who wanted autographs she smilingly signed "LBJ."

The month-long period of national mourning for President Kennedy ended on December twenty-second. By coincidence it was also Lady Bird's birthday, and after President Johnson spoke at a candlelight service at the Lincoln Memorial, the First Family went to the home of Lyndon's long-time administrative assistant, Walter Jenkins, for a quiet party celebration.

The guests, mostly Johnson staff aides, gathered around the gaily bedecked Christmas tree to present gifts to Lady Bird; and Lyndon surprised her with a portrait photograph of himself, on which he had inscribed the same words that he wrote on his first autographed picture to her twenty-nine years before: "For Bird, a girl of principles, ideals and refinement, from her admirer, Lyndon." It was a touching tribute after a month of grief and turmoil.

As they left the two-story frame house, a group of neighbors on the opposite curb began to sing, "Happy birthday, dear Lady Bird," and she blew them a kiss. "I want to thank you-all," she drawled, "and a happy Christmas to you."

The Johnsons went directly to the Ellipse behind the White House, where the new President lighted the nation's Christmas tree at the Pageant for Peace. They had planned to leave then for the ranch, but with Congress still stalled on the Foreign Aid Appropriations bill, Lyndon announced that he would remain in Washington until the House had acted.

The black crepe came down at the White House, and yuletide ornaments went up. A glittering Christmas tree, with crystal snowflakes and myriad balls and lights, now graced the oval Blue Room; and the next noon Lyndon suddenly decided that he wanted to invite every Senator and Representative to a White House party that afternoon. Such spur-of-the-moment decisions were nothing new to Bird, who gamely directed the setting up of two egg-nog bars in the East Room and state dining room, complete with fruitcake and steaming coffee.

The President had planned to have a pool of reporters cover the event for the rest of the White House contingent, but when Elizabeth Carpenter mentioned that women correspondents were coming at four o'clock to view the Christmas tree, he delightedly told her to have them stay for his party at five.

The party was one for the books. Disgruntled legislators, who were privately blaming the President for keeping them in session until Christmas Eve, nevertheless braved a six-inch snowstorm to make their way to the Executive Mansion. The President's house, they acknowledged, had never looked more loved and cared for. Besides the spruce and pine trees in the state rooms, holly decked the halls, colorful floral arrangements adorned the tables, a Southern kissing ball of mistletoe hung suspended from the crystal chandelier in the dining room, and Bird and her tall husband stood beside the Christmas tree to greet their guests.

They had warm words of appreciation, as well as handshakes, for the hastily invited Congressmen. Lyndon gave many of them his famed double-arm-grip treatment, and patted them on the back. Later, he climbed on a chair in the dining room to thank them for their efforts and pour a little oil on troubled waters.

After the last guest had departed, when nearly any President would gratefully have called it a day, LBJ suddenly invited four reporters who remained to accompany him on a tour of the swimming pool and his executive offices. Three years before, Bird had sagely observed that Lyndon's temperament was "not exactly suited to being the number two man." Now he was number one and obviously enjoying every minute of it. The old-time "Lyndon magic" was at work again, and once more "man had found job."

The House of Representatives met at the unprecedented hour of seven the next morning and passed the Foreign Aid bill without its restriction on wheat sales to Russia, which LBJ had vigorously opposed. The President, his wife, and daughter then flew to Philadelphia for the funeral of Representative William J. Green, Jr., and immediately afterward went on to Texas.

It was Christmas Eve, but the Johnsons were not yet free to join their assembled kinfolks at the ranch. Landing in Austin, they went directly to the governor's mansion to call on their old friend, John Connally, who was recuperating from the bullet wound sustained as he rode with the assassinated President exactly a month and a day before.

Now Christmas came at last to the Johnsons. Twenty-seven assorted relatives lounged around the living room and hallways, sniffing the fragrant aroma of turkey done to a crisp, as sixty reporters and photographers arrived to photograph the new President and his family.

With good-natured informality, the kissin' kin also trouped out to the sunny lawn for some group shots. The last "just one more" had been uttered by the photographers, when LBJ was seized with one of those spontaneous ideas that his wife had come to receive with an inward groan. How about, he said happily, showing the press through the house?

Smiling determinedly, Bird took his arm and soothed: "I think we're going to do all that on Friday." It was to no avail.

"They want to see what you've got in there for Christmas," Lyndon coaxed. "It won't take but a minute."

For twenty-nine years Lady Bird had known that it was useless to reason with her strong-willed husband when he was in that frame of mind. "As you say, darling," she sighed, and returned to her house guests.

While the President introduced sixty newsmen to his brother, sister, uncles, aunts, nephews, and cousins, the kinfolks cast anxious glances toward the kitchen. So did Lady Bird, who finally murmured, "That turkey and dressing is not getting any better." Lyndon heard her, but like Peck's Bad Boy gave no heed. He was having a marvelous time showing reporters a framed letter from Sam Houston to his great-grandfather, the fireplace made of native rock, the saddle from Mexican President Lopez Mateos, the dining-room set for twenty-eight places, and the Christmas tree. He tried the door to the bedroom, but it was locked.

"Mrs. Johnson has locked the bedroom on me," he exclaimed, but in a moment Bird graciously opened it. She had wanted to smooth the spreads. At last, Lyndon led the press tour outside, and the family breathed a sigh of relief. Now they could eat Christmas dinner. But not quite yet! As the President said good-bye and started back toward the house, he remembered a carton of ash trays with a map of the LBJ ranch and the Presidential seal on them. After an aide fetched them, he doled out the ash trays to each visitor, before returning to the now-dry turkey.

Lynda's fiancé, recently promoted from ensign to lieutenant junior grade, spent Christmas with the family, and Lyndon took it upon himself to inform newsmen that the destroyer to which Bernard Rosenbach was assigned would soon be leaving for Guantánamo Bay in Cuba. In fact, he was in an extremely confidential mood. He also revealed that Lucy's current beau, nineteen-year-old Jack Olsen of Maiden Rock, Wisconsin, who had spent Thanksgiving with them at "The Elms," was arriving the next day; and that he, Lyndon, had leased forty acres adjoining the ranch only that morning.

The next day Lady Bird busied herself with menus and arrangements for the weekend official visit of West German Chancellor Ludwig Erhard, and with a barbecue for the press. This was Thursday, and the following afternoon five busloads of newsmen and photographers arrived for a ranch-style barbecue and tour.

Wearing a green wool Marimekkos dress her husband had bought in Finland, a brown suede jacket, and an angelic smile, Bird hopped into one of the buses. Using a microphone, she then guided the reporters around the corrals, across the fields where new calves gamboled in the hazy overcast, and to the cemetery where nearly thirty Johnsons lay buried. After the press tour, the President used a makeshift podium concocted of two bales of hay to hold the first large news conference of his Administration. He was dressed all in brown, including his zippered jacket. His face was ruddy, and he looked the picture of health as he swung himself into the saddle of his walking horse, Lucy B., for the brief trip back to his beloved ranchhouse.

Lady Bird had provided a feast featuring barbecued spareribs and draft beer for the hundred and sixty newsmen, who had come from nearly every major country of the world, including Communist Russia and Poland. The menu was a foretaste of what Chancellor Erhard would sample on the morrow, and for him there would also be a German chocolate cake made from an old family recipe Bird had discovered in the Johnson files.

Nothing seemed too much trouble for Lady Bird during that first negotiating session between her Presidential husband and a foreign leader. The ranch office was turned over to Chancellor Erhard and his staff and the living area converted into conference rooms. As a consequence, LBJ's two secretaries, their typewriters and typing tables were moved to the foot of the Johnsons' bed in the master bedroom.

Lucy and Lynda gave up their spacious bedrooms to high-ranking German officials, and bunked together in a small one. All closets had to be cleared, and Erhard occupied the "best bedroom" overlooking the Pedernales River.

The inherited White House staff had submitted menus for meals, but when Bird saw Quiche Lorraine and other foreign dishes listed, she said practically: "Let's call that cheese custard pie and translate the others, too. That just sounds too fancy for Texas." She rejected flaming brandy desserts in favor of such homespun items as the German chocolate cake and Texas pecan pie. No foreign airs for Lady Bird.

She attended to every detail, both small and large. Learning from her Mayo physician, Dr. James Cain, that a member of the Mayo Clinic staff, Dr. James G. Connolly, was married to the daughter of Dr. Ludger Westrick, an economist accompanying Erhard to Texas, Bird wrote the Connollys a note inviting them to the festivities.

As Dr. Westrick stepped from the plane in Austin to greet his hosts, he gripped Bird's hand with special warmth and exclaimed: "You must be the most hospitable woman in the world. My daughter is coming, and I didn't even know that you knew of the relationship." Bird had also checked the American guest list with care, and on noting that State Senator Culp Krueger and Postmaster William Petmecky of nearby Fredericksburg were listed without their wives, she telephoned an invitation to the ladies.

She was constantly on tap as a chauffeur and guide for the visiting dignitaries. She also delegated German Assistant Foreign Secretary Franz Krapf as her "assistant host" to conduct tours of the ranch, as he had been there before. In fact, his wife, Helga, had been Bird's close friend during the years that Herr Krapf served as First Minister at the German Embassy in Washington.

Because most of the luncheons and dinners were for men only, Bird took her own meals with the entertainers and Presidential staff, "so they will feel more at home on such an official occasion." Worried that the children of staff members were feeling neglected, she arranged to have them taken to San Antonio to visit the Alamo and ride elephants at the zoo, while the barbecue was in progress.

By the time the rotund, food-loving Chancellor had partaken of that memorable chuck-wagon barbecue in the high-school gym at nearby Stonewall, he was ready to propose a heartfelt toast not only to the President but "to Mrs. Johnson, who created the restful, homelike atmosphere that made our talks, already due to be successful, even more so." The Texas guests could scarcely stop clapping at this tribute to the plantation-reared East Texas girl who had won the hearts of so many Americans and foreign visitors.

Like other wives faced with a rapid turnover of house guests, Bird had her private headaches. The logistics problem on sheets was becoming overwhelming, because the Johnson kinfolks, the German entourage, the Presidential staff, her own Taylor relatives, and such high-ranking American officials as Cabinet officers and Joint Chiefs of Staff were replacing each other in constant succession.

As Press Secretary Elizabeth Carpenter colorfully states it: "Every bed was being warmed every night, and the sheets had to be changed every morning." Soiled linens were dispatched regularly to the nearest laundry in Austin, sixty-five miles away, but the purchase of new sheets became an early chore.

Meanwhile, Lady Bird and her staff were busily engrossed in making plans for a performance of the Dutch Scappino Ballet at the White House the day after New Year's for underprivileged children from Northeast Settlement House, schools from Prince Georges County, Maryland, and the Merriweather Home.

The famous company had originally been invited by Mrs. Kennedy for a white House performance December eighteenth, but because of the mourning period Lady Bird had rescheduled it for January second. She could not be there in person, because the President was still working at the ranch, but she asked the wife of Secretary of State Dean Rusk to be her White House hostess for the gala children's party. She also thoughtfully added to the list all children of Netherlands Embassy personnel and the White House staff. It was a never-to-be-forgotten occasion for the two hundred moppets who shrieked at the antics of Scappino—in a ruffled collar and cocked hat—sipped ginger ale, and trailed cookie crumbs throughout the state rooms.

Lady Bird's brother, Antonio Taylor, his wife, and other Taylor relatives, including the widow of her brother, Tom Taylor, Jr., arrived at the ranch the day before New Year's. They all had a family dinner together, before the President flew to Austin to attend a New Year's Eve party given by his press contingent. Unfortunately, he did not return to the ranch in time to kiss his wife at the stroke of midnight, and usher in the brave new year.

Tony Taylor says of that evening with his sister and family: "We had a glorious watch-night party. Not the whoopee, ring-the-bells kind, but we sat around the open fireplace, praise be the saints, for a couple of hours and told tales. It was just good, sentimental talk, and I was in bed before midnight."

Tony was frankly worried about his beloved, overworked younger sister. "It seemed to me that Lyndon was feeling better than Lady Bird," he said. "He was not as restless as usual. He was in good health and good humor, but it seemed to me that Lady Bird was feeling the hectic pace. She would never say so, of course, but I added my voice to the chorus of the multitude, in urging her to get away quietly for some rest. She's been pictured as such a superwoman, and she is, but she can still get tired and worn out like the rest of us sometimes."

The Johnsons were marvelous hosts, as always. They took the Taylor kinfolks on their first ride in a helicopter to one of the adjoining ranches, and drove them to the frame cottage in Johnson City where the President had lived as a boy. Lady Bird had restored and redecorated it, in anticipation of making it available as a civic center for teas, Parent-Teachers meetings, and the like.

"Lyndon showed us the two old wooden mantlepieces," Tony recalled, "and he said it was pretty much as he remembered it, except that an open rear porch had been enclosed. It'll be a real nice civic center for a town the size of Johnson City."

Tony Taylor, who had been appointed by President Kennedy as a member of the Presidential Committee on Equal Opportunities, dutifully submitted his resignation when the changeover of administrations occurred, but his brother-in-law reminded him that he had requested all to remain at their posts.

LBJ invited Bird's brother to come to Washington in February to accompany him to his California meeting with Mexican President Lopez Mateos. When I asked Tony whether he hoped to sleep in the Lincoln bed, he grinned and said: "If I'm invited to, I think it would be quite an experience, and I would accept."

Reminded that Lincoln's ghost purportedly has been seen by White House occupants, Tony quipped: "He does have a spectral quality, with that stovepipe hat and long-tailed coat. I'm not afraid of ghosts in broad daylight. I don't know how I'd feel at midnight, but that wouldn't discourage me from sleeping in the Lincoln bed. Marse Abraham would intend me no harm."

Musing about the little sister who grew up to become First Lady, he said: "Naturally she has become more poised, better informed, and more understanding than a young person could be; but she has the same sense of values and the same humility. She could never be overbearing if she tried, but I think she's doing too much. I want her to rest."

On New Year's Day the Johnsons and Taylors sat down to a turkey dinner with all the trimmings, including the black-eyed peas that Southerners traditionally "eat for good luck" on January first.

Lynda Bird and Lucy Baines attended the Cotton Bowl football game in Dallas, but, because of the tragedy that had occurred in that city less than six weeks before, they were required by their unusually heavy Secret Service guard to remain incognito. Lynda, whose own University of Texas was playing the Academy sat on the Navy side as a gesture of loyalty to her absent fiancé; but Lucy chose the Texas side, to root for the home team. It was a foretaste of the security measures which will inhibit the gregarious girls as long as their father is President, for they were not even permitted to leave their seats during the half.

The President, who also had divided loyalties because of his wartime tour of duty with the Navy, watched the game on television. At twilight, Lady Bird piled her relatives into a station wagon and drove about the wild, wooded terrain of the ranch to watch the deer at play. It seemed an auspicious beginning for 1964.

The Taylor "kinfolks" departed the next day, and the parade of cabinet and sub-cabinet officers promptly resumed. There was no rest for either the President or the First Lady. While the former worked on his State of the Union and Budget Messages, his wife began preparations for her own busy schedule of entertainment and appointments.

They flew back to Washington Sunday evening with more house-guests in tow. Characteristically, they were LBJ's relatives rather than Bird's. The pace that the new First Lady set for women reporters during that first full week in the White House since the lifting of national mourning was a portent of "the shape of things to come."

She plunged immediately into arrangements for a Twelfth Night Christmas party for White House staffers and their spouses, and on Monday evening stood for two hours shaking more than a thousand hands. She had a personal word for each of them, from gardener to filing clerk. Disregarding her own weariness, she then went to the kitchen to greet those employees whose work had prevented their attendance at the festivities.

She conferred Tuesday with Genevieve Hendricks, the interior decorator who was refurbishing the two bedrooms which Lucy and Lynda inherited from John-John and Caroline Kennedy. Between times she helped welcome labor leaders and business executives who came in separate groups for a stag luncheon and stag dinner with the President. Her husband had resumed his eighteen-hour-a-day work schedule, and Bird saw him so fleetingly that she began pinning reminders about naps and resting on his bed-pillow, but the caution went unheeded.

Wednesday she went to the Capitol to hear LBJ's first State of the Union address to Congress, and that evening dropped in unexpectedly with him on a hundred-dollar-a-plate dinner given for their old friend, Senator Eugene J. McCarthy of Minnesota.

Thursday afternoon she stood with Mrs. Angier Biddle Duke, wife of the Chief of Protocol, to receive donors and workmen who had taken part in the restoration of Blair House, the President's guest house across the street from the White House.

The next afternoon she received sixty newswomen at a tea in the upstairs living quarters of the White House, and personally conducted them on a guided tour through the private rooms. It was sociability with a social conscience, however. Unwilling to waste such an opportunity, Lady Bird introduced Assistant Secretary of Labor Esther Peterson, the President's newly named adviser on consumer affairs, to talk about her hopes and plans. That evening she entertained with a gala teen-ager's party for Lucy Baines' friends.

During the week, she had been working on her speech for Wilkes College, and on Saturday she flew to the anthracite coal area of Pennsylvania for a whirlwind six-hour tour of projects designed to restore the economy of the stricken region. Although trailed by some fifty newswomen, she nevertheless established quick rapprochement with unemployed coal miners who were being re-trained for other work.

To a man who had been out of work for three years, before learning to be a house painter, she confided: "I do painting at my home on the ranch, and mix my own paints, too." Told that the technical institute offers re-training for men up to the age of fifty-five, because they are still considered productive, she laughingly remarked that she was glad to hear it. It was her husband's age.

Speaking to shivering crowds in the snow-covered squares of Scranton and Wilkes-Barre, she divorced her mission from politics by saying: "The problems here are not the problems of party. Poverty affects all of us. All must enlist in this war against poverty, and all of us must work together."

Welcoming placards called her "LBJ's Lady Bird," and miners' wives bubbled that it was the greatest day in their lives. When her hosts began comparing her with Eleanor Roosevelt, another energetic First Lady with highly developed social consciousness, Bird said simply: "I'd like to be as good as she was, but I have no feeling that I am."

There was no time for a pause in her schedule when she returned to the White House that evening. The President was entertaining members of the Democratic National Committee in the Blue Room, and within twenty minutes his wife had changed into a navy blue satin dress and was standing beside him in the receiving line.

A little later she slipped out with her husband to a waiting helicopter, and flew to Camp David for a chill week-end in the nearby Catoctin Mountains. They returned Sunday evening in a blinding snow storm. That was the week that was!

The next morning Lady Bird busied herself with multitudinous details for the glittering array of official parties that was to keep her engrossed in unpaid governmental duties well into the spring. President Antonio Segni of Italy and his Signora were arriving Tuesday, and the First Lady and the President met them at Union Station, riding with them in the first Parade since assuming office, and entertaining at a State Dinner that evening. The after-dinner Musicale ran the gamut from Italian opera to American hootenanny.

Luncheons were also being given at the White House during January for Canadian Prime Minister Lester Pearson and his wife, and for Queen Frederika of Greece. British Prime Minister Alec Douglas-Home was to be entertained at a White House luncheon on Lincoln's Birthday, and a week later President Lopez Mateos of Mexico would confer with President Johnson at Palm Springs, California. The annual White House receptions honoring Congress, the Judiciary, the Military, and the foreign Diplomatic Corps had also to be planned.

More than a quarter of a century before, Lady Bird Johnson had gamely permitted the Johnson abode in Austin to become a crossroads for every Texan who wanted to talk about the National Youth Administration. She had said of that period: "It was a real initiation into what the whole rest of my life was to be."

Now she was in charge of an historic mansion, which had become the crossroads of the world. It was a role that she had neither sought nor desired, but she brought to it unique capability, sweetness, and devotion. She had married a man of destiny, that she knew—and accepted.

Chapter

19

PRESIDENT Lyndon Baines Johnson is a highly complex individualist. A man of many moods, he soars to the heights one moment and plunges to the depths of gloom the next. He is a hard taskmaster, and his highly volatile nature seeks the nearest scapegoat when things go awry. Yet he is also a warmhearted, overly generous husband, father, and friend.

The President has an elephantine memory that never forgets a kindness. He is loyal, loving, and warm. He is uniquely attuned to his fellow man, which contributes to his remarkable powers of persuasion. No intellectual, he is nonetheless a brilliant man who commands fierce loyalty from his overworked staff. He is thin-skinned to a fault, where criticism is concerned, but he also proved his modesty during the three years that he stayed in the background as Vice-president.

In a word, Lyndon Johnson is many men, and his wife has learned to live with all of them. And what of Lady Bird herself? What of the shy Southern belle who through sheer determination converted herself into an outgoing, unaffected political campaigner and reigning hostess to the great of the world?

Perhaps the clue is found in the words of those who know her best. Mary Rather has said of her, "She is a total person." Liz Carpenter has described her as "a touch of velvet, with the stamina of steel." Her essence is described by Lynda Bird: "Sometimes, when Mother is away, I go into her room and smell her perfume and feel her presence."

With rare perception for a teenager, Lucy Baines puts it this way: "Mother is the calmest, most even-tempered person I know. When Daddy, Lynda and I get excited or upset over something, she pulls us all together. She's really the knot of our family. She can live through any difficult, trying time and never get mad, or lose her temper. She has complete control over her emotions. The rest of us have tempers, but Mother is a calm soul who smoothes us down, and makes all of us feel closer together."

And how does her husband describe this gentle wife? Says the President: "It is very difficult for me to talk about her with any degree of objectivity. She is a very warm, understanding person who is patient and enduring and always genuinely just. I never saw her slice a corner on anything. She has great character. She is the first to tell me about any mistakes, whether they are financial ventures or a political bonehead, and to me that is the test of real character.

"She has never lost any of the modesty and shyness she

had as a little girl. She is just as reluctant to be pushy at fifty-one as at fifteen, when she prayed every night that she wouldn't have to make that valedictory speech. She is the most enjoyable woman I have ever known.

"She is courageous, but not too adventurous. She doesn't like to get on a horse that she isn't sure of. She doesn't like to get used to new cars; she'd rather keep her old one. She doesn't like new clothes styles; I have a hard time getting her to change. She doesn't like a new cause. She has never lost a friend. I suppose the greatest attribute of all is that she can adjust herself to any situation, and do whatever it is well."

With typical modesty, Lady Bird says of herself: "There is so much more that I ought to do. My appetite is bigger than my strength—my appetite for information and for contribution."

Bird has quaintly said of her husband: "Lyndon stretches you." She explains her meaning in this fashion: "He always expects more of you than you're really mentally or physically capable of putting out. Somehow that makes you try a little bit harder, and makes you produce a little more. It is really a very good fertilizer for growth; it's also very tiring."

With a quizzical smile she continued: "For instance, he's always expecting me to look better than I do, which means that I have to make up in grooming, buying clothes, and taking exercises for what doesn't happen naturally. Sometimes I rebel against it, and I'm a little annoyed with being so materialistic about looks; but every time I see somebody my own age and imagine that I look or act a little younger —which is probably utterly ridiculous—I know that I must give Lyndon the credit, because he has prodded me into doing things that do not come naturally for me."

Bird frankly concedes that she was "a much less gregarious, outgoing person" before she married Lyndon. "He has made me realize that it's more fun to have your life touch the lives of a lot of others with human warmth, so if I have any more friends I must give him a lot of credit for that, too."

The sweetness of Lady Bird's nature was never more apparent than in the statement she made when moving to the White House. "I will try," she said, "to be a balm, sustainer, and sometimes a critic for my husband; to help my children look at this job with all the reverence it is due, to get from it the knowledge their unique vantage point gives them, and to retain the lightheartedness to which every teenager is entitled. For my own self, my role must emerge in deeds, not words."

Only a few weeks before the tragedy in Dallas that so abruptly changed her life, she spoke of the things that she enjoyed most. Characteristically, they were simple pleasures that bespeak her kinship with the American tradition. In her soft Southern drawl, she began: "I like being real tired from getting the last weed out of the zinnia bed, and finally sitting down with a glass of lemonade to see how pretty the flowers look. I like sitting on the back of the boat at twilight, down home on the Llano River, watching the sun go down behind Pack Saddle Mountain. If that won't bring joy to your soul, you're past saving.

"Then there's the joy of getting your desk clean, and knowing that all your letters are answered, and you can see the wood on it again. There's something real satisfying about working, and having gotten it done. And there's something equally satisfying about just sitting around the kitchen table and having a glass of milk with Lynda Bird, while she tells me all her problems, and I feel that we've gotten to that intimate little moment of true meeting. Those are the times when I am really happy."

Such times may now be few and far between for the busy First Lady. Of her new role, she has said: "I feel as if I'm suddenly on stage for a part I never rehearsed, but like Lyndon I will do my best."

A few weeks after she had assumed that unrehearsed part, we sat chatting together in her bedroom at the White House. "My first job," she said pensively, "is to make this home a place where Lyndon can operate productively, and to add to his operation in every way that I can, because I have never felt so much need on his part, and so much compassion on my part for him.

"My second job is to enjoy and share it with Lucy and Lynda, for this is an opportunity as well as a responsibility. Because the children are now sixteen and nineteen, the time will approach when I will have extra time to devote myself to what I hope will be constructive things.

"My job as First Lady will have to grow and come into being. I don't think that I'll be arid of thoughts, and I hope that I won't be arid of achievements, but the important thing is to help Lyndon all that we can. I look forward to having the companionship and help of Lynda Bird, since we've persuaded her to transfer to Washington for her second term this year."

Taking an analytical look backward at her three years as Second Lady, she decided that: "The things I enjoyed most were participating in the rich fiber of our country:

getting to know the youngsters who were going to Chile on scholarships, the members of COPE who were here on convention, the high-school home economics teachers who came to Washington to learn new techniques, the postal-service employees who came out one snowy afternoon, all the ladies from the United Nations who came down from New York. The world has opened up to me during these three years, and I enjoyed the overseas travels, too; but I don't know how much of that will be possible now."

Lucy Baines returned from school, and came in to kiss her mother. The talk turned to her father, and the school-girl said of him: "He has the most excellent taste in clothes of any man I've ever seen. When he comes back from a trip he always brings something that is just precious, something that we had imagined all the time but never could have found in a store.

"Daddy has an objection to certain kinds of clothes—real bulky things and pleated skirts—and we say, 'Daddy, they're fashionable and they look good, and we like them.' But he says, 'I like this.' We reply, 'Well, we can't find it'; but inevitably he does find what he's talking about. He brings it back, and it looks so sharp that there's nothing else we can say. He never forgets. I've never known him to go on a trip for any length of time that he didn't bring us something back that was real personal and real cute.

"When he went abroad this summer, he brought me back lots and lots of little things. Nothing big, but articles of clothing, and every single one of them fit!" Lady Bird sat beaming proudly until Lucy, who likes to cook, disappeared into the second floor "family" kitchen to bake cookies.

We talked on quietly for a time, and then I asked the

First Lady where she would eventually like to live, after the turmoil and excitement of the Presidency are past.

A faraway look crept into her eyes, and she began pensively: "If one can speak with assurance about anything—and certainly the last weeks have shown us that we can't—I know that I will go on to Texas, livin' or dead, to the ranch. At least I earnestly believe that I will. It would be nice also to have a comfortable small house in Austin, but the ranch will be our home."

This was, of course, the LBJ ranch, of which the President has said: "It's the sort of place where they love you while you're alive; they take care of you when you're sick; and they miss you when you're dead."

The ranch, as Lady Bird has so aptly put it, is "our heart's home." If this modest, unassuming woman has her way, the epitaph on her tombstone might someday read:

From the "Brick House" to the White House to the ranchhouse.

Chapter
20

THE PALE WINTER twilight had long since faded into dusk, and the spotlighted White House glittered like a diamond-encrusted pendant on the twinkling chain formed by the length of Pennsylvania Avenue.

The bumper-to-bumper crush of rush-hour traffic had completed its honking, homeward crawl. Storekeepers, file clerks, and industrial tycoons, having thrust aside their workaday problems, were by now easing into house slippers, or dressing for a gay evening on the town.

Not so the President of the United States. The big man in the lonely job had been engrossed in the problems of the world from the moment that he swung his long legs out of bed at six-thirty that morning. Not until three o'clock in the afternoon had he found time for a midday snack.

Violence was flaring in Panama, and he had expeditiously dispatched a blue-ribbon group of Latin American experts to the trouble spot. He had been on the telephone frequently with top advisers throughout the hectic day, and was consequently running more than an hour behind in his schedule of appointments.

It was a quarter to seven when he strode out of the oval Presidential office, laid a friendly arm across my shoulders, and escorted me inside. Disregarding his own cares and stresses, he was full of apologies for a possible inconvenience to me. Would I like coffee or an orange drink?

A white-coated attendant brought two tall glasses of orange soda, and after the President had asked me to be seated, he pulled forward his own high-backed rocker. We were ready, then, to talk about his favorite subject—Lady Bird.

"I don't know that it will look well for me to be blowing the horn about her," he said with a boyish grin, "but you can't get anything very objective out of me on that subject." The active President mused for a moment, and began thoughtfully: "No one has ever had to carry a load for her in her life. She has just never stepped in the mud, and had to be lifted out. She is one of the best planners, best organizers, and best directors ever born.

"She's one of the few people who never feels sorry for herself. No matter how complicated things get, she never feels that she's being imposed upon. She never loses her dignity. She's a lady. If she disapproves of something you say, she never says so, but she somehow makes you want to correct it yourself. She won't argue. You can't get an argument out of her, because she's above it all."

The President took a swallow of orange soda, and continued: "As a companion she has no equal. She's soft and kind and understanding. She's always willing to meet you more than halfway. If you want to ride and she wants to walk, she'll ride. If she wants a fire in the living room and you don't, she says sweetly, 'We'll have it some other time.'

"She's wonderful with our children. I've never heard her correct either of them. Once she suggested a curfew, but Lucy said it would make her feel as if she wasn't trusted, to have to watch the clock and leave three minutes before the hour. Her mother laughed with her over that, and concluded that Lucy might be right. She said we'd try it that way for a while, and from then on there's been no curfew. The girls know that they are trusted."

The telephone rang, and the President accepted a call from one of the highest officials in our government. His mind quickly grasped the problem and he unhesitatingly supplied the name of the man who had the required information. Then he leaned back in the rocker, and picked up the thread of our conversation as if there had been no interruption.

"Lady Bird," he said, "is the soul of efficiency. When she comes in to see me, she has maybe five things jotted down, which she presents in logical and orderly fashion. She is very executive in her approach to problems. She always puts others' interests above her own. For instance, our first house guests at the White House are not rich people, and they're not Bird's relatives. They're my eighty-year-old uncle, Huffman Baines, and his wife, and my mother's only sister, Mrs. Josefa Saunders."

The President looked the picture of a healthy, contented man who has everything that the heart desires. Making it plain that he still considers his life partner the best "date" that any man could want, he pointed out that Bird likes to swim and dance; she is gay, beguiling, and intelligent.

"As a companion, she's the best," he declared, "and as a housekeeper she's perfection. She runs a house just like she would a well-managed hotel. Your clothes are always in place. They are sent to the cleaners when they need to be, and they are ready when you want them. As a mother . . . well, in my opinion no mother in the world could do a better job than she does of managing children.

"Her children love her as a companion. They never regard her as a chaperone, but are excited and happy when she is going to one of their parties. The boys who hang around our house have always been crazy about her. They confide in her more than anyone, because she's the kind of person that you want to talk to."

An appreciative glow lighted his dark brown eyes, and he said feelingly: "She's the most generous person in the world, yet she never makes anyone feel indebted to her. After she borrowed that ten-thousand-dollar advance from her father against her inheritance, to finance my first Congressional campaign, all she ever said about it was: 'Why don't we set aside five hundred dollars a month out of the paycheck to rebuild the fund, so that we'll have it again when we need it?'

"Lady Bird is very high on my associates—all the men and women who work for me. At a White House party the other day, she invited my Secretary and my newest Assistant, right along with the Chief Justice. At my first address to a Joint Session, she had Zephyr with her in the family gallery, and for the State of the Union message, Helen Williams." Zephyr Wright is the Johnson's long-time cook, and Helen Williams is the housekeeper who came to work as the children's nursemaid when Lucy was a toddler.

The squawkbox sounded, and the President handled the query. He took another sip of his orange soda, and, rocking back, remarked that he has always marveled at Bird's genuine enjoyment of formal dinners.

"She's a great admirer of Adlai Stevenson," he confided, "and she also loves to talk to such diverse dinner partners as Senators Hubert Humphrey, Eugene McCarthy, and Dick Russell. They are very different types of personalities. After a hard day's work, I've never been too keen on dinner parties, and I once asked her how she managed to have such a good time. She explained that she usually asks her dinner partner some question about himself, and that she enjoys listening as much as he enjoys answering. That's pretty smart."

The President was patently proud of the way his wife can adapt herself to any situation or to any caller. He said she is equally as comfortable with Queen Frederika of Greece or President Charles De Gaulle of France as with a visitor from Texas.

"She's a woman of great depth and excellent judgment." He beamed. "I never ask her opinion but that she doesn't help with constructive criticism. Take my State of the Union message, for instance. She worked on it with me beforehand. It was the shortest such message in three decades, but it took forty-one minutes to read because it was interrupted eighty-one times by applause, which set some kind of a record. Afterward, Bird told me something constructive. She said she thought that I read it a little too slowly, and she's undoubtedly right."

A note of pride crept into his voice as he declared:

"She's a great reader. She knows the classics and history, and it's therefore easy for her to dip into any century and come up with some good illustration to confirm the wisdom of judging the future by the past.

"She's an excellent businesswoman, a good counsellor and guide to her children. She has trained them so well that they can make out their own income-tax reports. Lynda has worked every summer at KTBC, and has learned nearly every department from copy girl to receptionist to accountant.

"Their mother inspired them to like studying, and although the Cathedral School is hard work scholastically, they both are sold on it. Since her graduation there, Lynda has been on the honor roll at the University of Texas, and Lucy will be, when she goes to college. Lucy eats her dinner every night at six o'clock. When I try to persuade her to wait and eat with us at seven-thirty or eight, she says she can't because she has to get to her books. As soon as she finishes dinner, she studies until eleven or twelve o'clock. Once I found one of her schoolbooks in the treaty room, when I was showing some visitors through.

"Bird has taught the girls to be independent. They manage their allowances and buy their own clothes. The other day, Lucy went out and bought four or five dresses that she needed. I heard her telling her mother that she had spent eight dollars for this one, and twelve dollars for that. The girls have inherited their mother's thrift."

When I laughingly remarked that they "all seemed to have that quality except Papa," the President grinned broadly, showing the deeply etched dimples which Lynda has inherited.

"I practice thrift when it comes to family money—and the government's," he amended. "Maybe I'm apt to loosen up a little bit when it comes to my own."

It was past the dinner hour, but other callers still waited their turn in the cavernous reception room next door. The President, relaxed and charming, had not once been so ungracious as to glance at the clock. It was I who apologetically noted the passage of time and rose to leave.

The Chief Executive strolled with me across the broad expanse of the room, still talking. As we passed the huge Presidential desk, his eye caught a large batch of photographs stacked there.

Mr. Johnson lifted a picture from the top of the stack, and we silently studied it together. It was a classic, unposed picture of the man who now guides this nation's destiny. His back was to the camera, and his lean, rangy figure was silhouetted against the white colonnades of the walkway as he strode from his office to the adjoining Executive Mansion. Night had obviously fallen, and the President's sole companion seemed to be his little beagle.

"The loneliest man in the world," LBJ observed, with a deprecatory smile.

Lyndon Baines Johnson, the President of the United States, is necessarily that; yet Lyndon Baines Johnson, the man, is not. It requires little imagination for those who truly know him to picture the scene which occurred soon after the camera had recorded that eloquent moment in time.

LBJ would walk into the White House family quarters and remark automatically to the first person within earshot: "Where's Bird?"

As always, his devoted wife would be near enough to reply in person: "Right here, darling."

Acknowledgments

Mrs. LBJ is the culmination of twenty years of friendship with a truly remarkable woman—Lady Bird Johnson. I should like to express my sincere gratitude for her generous co-operation, which has helped to make this book possible.

I am particularly appreciative of the valuable time which the busy First Lady has devoted to filling the gaps in my knowledge about her early years, confiding the sentiments and inner thoughts of the mature woman; and proofreading my manuscript in order to avoid the possibility of error.

Thanks to her vivid recall and painstaking eye for detail, I am privileged to present this authentic life story of a charming First Lady. Those who know her will agree that she is notable not only for her intelligence, devotion to duty, and zest for living; but also for her winsome femininity, her warmheartedness, and poetic turn of phrase.

I am deeply grateful to President Johnson who, although absorbed with his awesome new responsibilities, nonetheless evinced keen interest in the project and blocked off time for me in his heavy schedule of appointments.

Much of the richness of detail was provided by Elizabeth Carpenter, Mrs. Johnson's press secretary, and by Mary Rather of Hillsboro, Texas, both of whom are intimate friends of the Johnson family. Their assistance has proved invaluable in projecting a well-rounded word portrait of a motherless Southern girl who became the chatelaine of the White House.

I should also like to acknowledge my indebtedness to Antonio Taylor of Santa Fe, the First Lady's only surviving brother; and to Ann Worley; "Scooter" Miller; Willie Day Taylor; Blake Clark; Leslie Carpenter; and Bess Abell, the White House Social Secretary. These friends and relatives gladly dipped into their precious storehouse of memories in order to share their experiences.